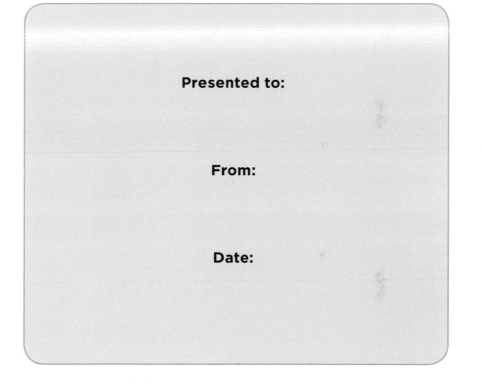

Presented to:

From:

Date:

# BOOKS BY GARY THOMAS

# DEVOTIONS

*for*

# SACRED
# PARENTING

# GARY THOMAS

ZONDERVAN®

ZONDERVAN

*Devotions for Sacred Parenting*

Copyright © 2005, 2018 by Gary L. Thomas

Published in Grand Rapids, Michigan, by Zondervan. Zondervan is a registered trademark of The Zondervan Corporation, L.L.C., a wholly owned subsidiary of HarperCollins Christian Publishing, Inc.

Requests for information should be addressed to customercare@harpercollins.com.

ISBN 978-0-3104-1582-4 (audiobook)
ISBN 978-0-3100-9070-0 (eBook)
ISBN 978-0-3100-9069-4 (HC)

*Cover design: Left Coast Design*
*Interior design: Kenny Holcomb*

*Printed in China*

23 24 25 26 27 28 29 / DSC / 16 15 14 13 12 11 10 9 8 7 6 5 4 3

**FOR
JOHN
SLOAN**

I thought I had found an editor and instead found a friend.
John has worked for years as a partner in this writing
ministry. He lives one of those wonderful "quiet but godly"
lives. You'll be hearing much more about him in heaven.

# CONTENTS

# CONTENTS

# CONTENTS

# GOD IS IN THE ROOM

*Where can I go from your Spirit?*
*Where can I flee from your presence?*
*If I go up to the heavens, you are there;*
*if I make my bed in the depths, you are there.*
*If I rise on the wings of the dawn,*
*if I settle on the far side of the sea,*
*even there your hand will guide me,*
*your right hand will hold me fast.*

PSALM 139:7–10

I'D LIKE TO SUGGEST A MOTTO FOR CHRISTIAN FAMILY LIFE: "God is in the room."

While God is *always* there, so often we act and think and behave and speak as if he were not. We fight, we argue, we laugh; we play games, watch movies, make love, and do just about everything without even thinking about the implication that *God is in the room.*

Even though we pray before our common meals, it amazes me how quickly I can slip back into thinking and acting as if the word *Amen* is a kind of curtain that I pull down in front of heaven. I've said my obligatory piece, and now I can carry on as if God has passed over us rather than taken up residence among us.

Think of how differently we might treat our children in those frustrating moments if we responded to them with the knowledge that God is in the room. If we truly believed that the God who designed them and who is passionate about their welfare was literally looking over our shoulders, might we be a little more patient, a little more understanding?

Would we discipline our kids a little differently? Would we pay them more attention?

It's such a simple notion, but it can be so revolutionary: *God is in the room!*

I don't know about you, but I seriously doubt I would so casually raise my voice, or be quite so selfish or lazy if I could see God sitting in my kitchen or living room. Above all, I'd want my children to notice him and acknowledge him, and I think I'd be more likely to focus on the kind of parenting that would please him at any given moment. I'd look to him for encouragement when a child seemed disheartened. I'd ask his advice when a child sought my counsel. I imagine that after doing or saying anything, I'd want to look at him to read his expression.

This would be a blessing, not a burden, and it's something we can begin to practice. A women's group that I spoke to made up plaques: "God is in the Room" that they sold so that members could post them in their homes as a constant reminder.

How would parenting change if we talked as if God were in the room? "Honey, how do you think God feels about your attitude right now? Is this pleasing to him?" "I know you're afraid, but God's here, in this house. He really is. And he's watching over all of us, so you can sleep peacefully."

Tell it to yourself, every morning, every noontime, every evening: God is in the room.

Tell it to each other, every time you're tempted to yell, or criticize, or ridicule, or even ignore each other: God is in the room.

Tell it to your children, throughout the day: God is in the room.

Let's keep telling it to ourselves and to each other until we practice it and live it, until we live and breathe with the blessed remembrance: God is in the room.

*God is in the room.*

> *Heavenly Father, because you are a loving God, we are so blessed to know that you are always in the room. Let us remember you with worshipful hearts and appropriate reverence. Help us to pass this same awareness on to our children. In Jesus' name, amen.*

## Questions for Reflection

1. Think of two or three things you can do to remind yourself in the coming weeks that God is in the room.
2. Think back over the past week. What might you have done differently had you been able to see that God was in the room?

# 2

# THE RIGHT PERSON
# FOR THE JOB

*But now, this is what the L*ORD *says—*
*he who created you, Jacob,*
*he who formed you, Israel:*
*"Do not fear, for I have redeemed you;*
*I have summoned you by name; you are mine."*

ISAIAH 43:1

IF YOU WERE TO ASK MOST SEMINARY PROFESSORS TO NAME the top ten preachers of all time, on the vast majority of those lists—if not on *all*—would undoubtedly fall the name Charles Haddon Spurgeon (1834–1892), the celebrated Baptist often referred to as the "prince of preachers." His sermons became so popular his church had to build a tabernacle that could seat the six thousand people who wanted to hear him, and many leading newspapers around the world (Spurgeon ministered in London) printed weekly transcripts of his messages.

And yet in one sermon Spurgeon made an astonishing confession: "I have been lamenting my unfitness for my work."[1]

Who could imagine that Spurgeon, one of the most successful ever at his position, could feel inadequate for a task at which he clearly excelled?

And yet I meet many involved and capable parents who feel the same way. "Maybe," they think, "I'm just not up to the task. Parenting asks of me skills and wisdom and energy I just don't possess."

Have you ever been there?

The Great Discourager, Satan, has a way of distracting us with pernicious questions: "Who are *you* to raise a child? What makes you think that *you*, of all people, can be a parent? These children would be better off without you!"

Spurgeon found hope in Isaiah 43:1: "But now, this is what the LORD says—he who created you, Jacob, he who formed you, Israel: 'Do not fear, for I have redeemed you; I have summoned you by name; you are mine.'"

Spurgeon explains, "I said to myself, 'I am what God created me to be, and I am what He formed me to be. Therefore, I must, after all, be the right man for the place in which He has put me.'"[2]

God not only created you; he created your children. And he chose to place those children in *your* home. To doubt any of this is to question the sovereignty of God. Do you think God doesn't care for your children? Do you imagine your son or daughter to be a mere afterthought who somehow escaped God's attention? Not a chance! God designed your children, and he placed them in your care.

To win a war, you need to know not only your objective but also your enemy. The ancients didn't shy away from talking about Satan—as we often do today—and they knew his tactics, chief among them being discouragement. If Satan can't entice us to neglect our duties, he'll work overtime to *discourage* us in them.

If your discouragement stems from perplexity—not knowing what to do—we find comfort in our Savior. Spurgeon said that if God could figure out how to be just and yet save sinners, if he could find a way to declare his war against evil while still forgiving sin, surely he can solve *our* challenges! There never was, nor ever will be, a problem so perplexing that God's guidance can't see us through it.

If we worry about what we lack, financially or in personal abilities, we find comfort in God's promise: "He who did not spare his own Son, but gave him up for us all—how will he not also, along with him, graciously give us all things?" (Romans 8:32).

Whatever our personal cause of discouragement, God has provided an ironclad cure. Spurgeon observed, "With the bloodstain upon us, we may well cease to fear. . . . How can we be deserted in the hour of need? We have been bought with too great a price for our Redeemer to let us slip. Therefore, let us march on with confidence."[3]

The stakes you face as a parent are much too great to go unnoticed by a God who loves you and your children so much that he didn't spare his own Son in his zeal to redeem you. The God who did that is the God who watches over you now, the same God who inspired Spurgeon to offer this sermon more than a hundred years ago and who inspired you to pick up this book to hear these words anew.

You *are* the right person for the job, because God himself has assigned you the task. And he is committed to seeing you through.

In the end, that's all we need to know.

*Heavenly Father, thank you for choosing us and placing our children under our care. Help us to take comfort in your sovereignty and to know that you would never assign to us a task without giving us all that we need to complete it. Protect us from Satan's discouragement, and give us hope that you will bless our children as we seek to honor you. In Jesus' name, amen.*

## Questions for Reflection

1. What do you feel you lack most as a parent? Time? Money? Wisdom? Energy? Something else?

2. How can reminding yourself of God's sovereignty—that he put your children into your care—encourage you in your task?

3. List two or three positive reasons for why you think God might have wanted you to raise your particular children. How has he uniquely gifted you to bless these children with their particular needs?

# A LASTING MARK

*Whoever who fears the LORD has a secure fortress,*
*and for their children it will be a refuge.*

PROVERBS 14:26

IN A WORLD WHERE TWO DIFFERENT NEWS STATIONS CAN PRO-
vide two opposing sets of facts as the truth, it's easy to throw up our
hands and say, "It's chaos! Nobody really knows the truth." We want to
know the truth, but when two different people give us two different sets
of facts, it actually feels like a relief to find a reliable, trusted source.

That's what it's like for a child trying to determine her values.
Chaos surrounds our kids; they need a mom and a dad to walk before
them to show them the way. They need to see how we, overwhelmed
by life, find security and hope in a God who is greater than we are,
and how we strive to live unselfishly, even sacrificially when need be,
to seek first the kingdom of God. We model an appropriate fear of the
Lord—reverencing him, obeying his Word, walking in his ways—and
cultivate a hatred for sin. When we do this, we construct a spiritual refuge for our children. Proverbs 14:26 tells us, "Whoever fears the LORD
has a secure fortress, and *for their children* it will be a refuge" (emphasis
added). That's right—our walking in the fear of God becomes a refuge
for our children.

As a single man, I looked at righteousness self-centeredly—how my choices would affect my standing with God, how moral decisions might affect my future and sense of well-being. But as a parent, I must consider the possible generational consequences. Andrew Murray puts it this way: "In all God's dealings with us in redemption and grace, in His revelation in Christ and His cross, He has one goal—to save us from sin and make us partakers of His holiness. If the parent is to be God's fellow-worker, . . . the parent himself must be in harmony with God. He must hate sin with a perfect hatred and seek above everything to remove and keep it out of his home."[1]

Every time a man talks to his son about women, he creates a moral example—will he be in harmony with God, or will he adopt the prejudicial mind-set of this age?

Every time a woman speaks of her husband in front of her children, she creates a moral example—will it be a good one or a negative one?

Every time a man sits in front of a computer and logs onto the Internet, he creates a moral trail—will he hate sin "with a perfect hatred and seek above everything to remove and keep it out of his home," or will he allow it to infiltrate his children's abode?

Every time parents face the struggle to choose nurturing care over personal fulfillment, they create a moral trail—will their priorities be in harmony with God, or will they be governed by fear of what others may think?

When our kids see how we deal with failure, disappointment, frustration, and our own limitations, they are learning. Are we building a secure refuge, or will it be a shoddy cardboard house that won't make it through a single storm? Do they witness a faith that will last through cancer, unemployment, frustration, and stress, or are they looking at a belief that wilts under the slightest spiritual assault?

There's an unavoidable truth behind all this: just as God created man and woman in his own image, so we parents end up creating boys and girls very much in *our* image. As Jesus said, "Everyone who is fully trained will be like their teacher" (Luke 6:40).

None of us, of course, leave a *perfect* example. But that doesn't mean we can't leave an influential one. My desire—my goal—is that my children will see the joy and meaning and purpose that come from seeking first the kingdom of God, making anything that this world offers pale by comparison. In Andrew Murray's words, "The parent must present to the child the beauty of virtue, the nobility and happiness of self-denial, the pleasure that duty brings, and the fear and the favor of God."[2]

I love Murray's quote because it presents the positive side of living out these precious truths in front of our children. Virtue, though often mocked and ridiculed, is as beautiful as wickedness is ugly. Self-denial curiously spawns joyful happiness, while selfishness and arrogance produce desperation and obsession. Being faithful to duty brings great fulfillment, while following unchecked passions eventually leads us to despise ourselves. And the greatest truth of all: there is no higher end, no more glorious life, no better aim, than to live in the fear and favor of almighty God.

Paul certainly understood parenting in this way: "For you know that we dealt with each of you as a father deals with his own children, encouraging, comforting and urging you to live lives worthy of God, who calls you into his kingdom and glory" (1 Thessalonians 2:11–12). Paul quite simply *assumed* that parents will live this way—encouraging their children to live lives "worthy of God."

What kind of example are we leaving behind today?

*Heavenly Father, one of our highest aims is that our children*
*would see you and your ways as a refuge, a shelter, a shield.*
*Give us a new thirst for righteousness, help us grow in holiness,*
*and help us to make faith a compelling invitation that our kids*
*can't wait to receive for themselves. In Jesus' name, amen.*

## Questions for Reflection

1. Do the two of you leave one complementary example to your children, celebrating faith and obedience, or are there areas where your children might receive mixed messages? If it's the latter, what can you do to get on the same page?

2. How can parents help children understand the "beauty of virtue," as well as the "nobility and happiness of self-denial"? Pray through some of the ways you can make true faith even more compelling to your children.

3. Where do you need to grow personally in order to live a life "worthy of God" according to 1 Thessalonians 2:11–12?

# 4

# BRINGING JOY TO OUR HEAVENLY FATHER

*I have no greater joy than to hear that my
children are walking in the truth.*

3 John 4

At an end-of-the-season sports banquet, my son and his teammates slipped out of the restaurant where we had been eating pizza and went next door to a video store to scope out some of the newest video games. About five minutes later, Graham returned to the restaurant, alone. We thought it odd that Graham came back early, all by himself, but didn't say anything about it.

When we got home, we found out what had happened. After checking out the video games, one of the boys said, "Hey, let's go look for dirty covers on the movies." The rest of the team fell into line; Graham said no and slipped out of the store, on his own.

I felt my heart swell with affection for Graham when I heard the story. We had been having a series of lunches discussing a hundred-year-old book, J. C. Ryle's *Thoughts for Young Men,* in which Ryle warns of a young man's temptations. It so encouraged me to see Graham taking this teaching to heart. I felt far more proud of him for this than for his outstanding play in the championship game.

The next day, I had to leave for a cross-country trip. As I prayed in the early morning hours on my drive to the airport, God brought back to my mind the affection I had felt over Graham. I believe he was suggesting that that's how *he* feels when we adults walk away from temptation. Our temptations may differ from those of our children, but the spiritual pressure is just as real and the consequences just as severe. When God sees an adult son or daughter face such temptation and *walk away*, his heart likewise swells with affection.

I'm not suggesting that God loves us *more* based on our behavior but that we can bring special satisfaction to our heavenly Father by living obedient lives. I am so attuned to disappointing God when I fail, so acutely aware of how much pain I cause him when I mess up, that it felt quite refreshing to think that when I walk away from temptation, I bring him great pleasure.

The apostle John wrote that nothing gave him more pleasure than to hear that his children were walking in the truth. I believe he modeled the father heart of God when he said this. As parents, we can certainly attest to this truth with our own kids.

Today, you will have opportunities to bring pleasure to God. So often, when we consider sin, we think of negative consequences: getting found out, landing in trouble, facing God's wrath. But just for once, why don't we consider the *positive* consequences of obedience that bring joy to our heavenly Father? Let's put a smile on God's face. Let's bring him great happiness.

When you walk away from an infatuation and choose to stay faithful to your marriage, you make God happy.

When you do your work with integrity and treat your business as if God himself were reviewing your records, you put a smile on his face.

When you take the time to encourage someone, when you help someone who needs a hand, when you stop gossip cold in its tracks, you make God proud and bring him great joy.

What a way to look at the day! I can make God smile. I can make God proud. I can bring God great joy!

Let's get started.

*Heavenly Father, your forgiveness and grace have filled us with such pleasure; how amazing it is to think that something we do can bring pleasure back to you. Give us a new hunger to live obedient lives so that we might make you smile. In Jesus' name, amen.*

## Questions for Reflection

1. Discuss a time when your child's obedience made you especially happy. What did that child do, and how did it make you feel?
2. What challenge are you facing today that gains new perspective when you think about what will make God happiest? How do you now think you should respond?

# 5

# BRING THE BOY TO ME

*And what does the one God seek? Godly offspring.*
MALACHI 2:15

THE ROYAL SERVANT OBADIAH TOLD THE PROPHET ELIJAH, "I your servant have worshiped the LORD since my youth" (1 Kings 18:12). It seems likely from this confession, and from his name, that Obadiah must have had believing parents. Obadiah means "servant of Yahweh [the LORD]"—this in a time when Ahab and Jezebel made killing the Lord's prophets a royal blood sport. Any parent wanting to curry favor with the prevailing royal court wouldn't have dared to label their son with such a name. Instead, they'd choose "servant of Baal" or "follower of Chemosh" (or some other false god touted by Jezebel). But Obadiah's parents chose "servant of Yahweh," and their boy proved it was more than just a name. During the great persecution, Obadiah used his influence to courageously hide a hundred prophets of the living God, whom he fed and gave water to until the pogrom had passed.[1]

Obadiah's life provides a true parable of the prophetic nature behind having kids. People choose to have children (or not to have children) for the flimsiest of reasons: carrying on the family name, a desire to experience the intimate parent-child relationship, because we want someone there for us in our old age, because we fear we would feel lonely without children—and our future actions as parents will be shaped by these purposes. If my goal is simply to raise "happy" children, I'll buy them whatever they want instead of teaching them to be responsible and caring with money. If my goal is to have "successful" children, I will spare no expense helping them to rise above others—they'll get the best coaching, the best equipment, maybe even the services of a sports psychologist. I'll act as if the most important thing in the world is that they get in the right school, with the right classes and the right diplomas, so they can get a job with the right company in the right industry.

But Christian parenting calls us to a much different purpose and motivation: raising servants of Yahweh. Malachi tells us that God became angry with the people of Israel and refused to accept their prayers or offerings because they were breaking the covenant of marriage. And yet, in the context of Malachi's words, it doesn't appear God had in mind the preservation of marriage for marriage's sake; in this instance, marriage seems to be the means to another end: "Has not the one God made you? You belong to him in body and spirit. And what does the one God seek? *Godly offspring.* So be on your guard, and do not be unfaithful to the wife of your youth" (Malachi 2:15, emphasis added).

God wants us to maintain our marriages because he desires that we have *godly* offspring. Having children isn't the only purpose of marriage, of course, but it is certainly a primary one. God wants us to keep our marriages together so we don't sabotage this aim. Godly marriages are far more likely to produce godly children. Unstable, chaotic, and "serial" marriages often produce troubled kids—and that's not the kind of offering God wants from us.

Malachi also gives us a picture of what a godly child is: "[Levi] revered me and stood in awe of my name. True instruction was in his mouth and nothing false was found on his lips. He walked with me in peace and uprightness, and turned many from sin" (Malachi 2:5–6).

According to this passage, God wants us to maintain families that teach our daughters and sons to

- live in awe of him;
- revere his Word;
- walk with him in fellowship;
- live peacefully with others; and
- turn others from their sins.

In other words, *God wants us to raise faithful servants.*

When I seek to raise children for the glory of God, when I figuratively declare my children "Obadiahs"—servants of the Lord—I'll be willing to face the difficult realities of training, correcting, encouraging, praying, and so forth, because I know there's no higher end, no more important use of my time, no greater good, than that I should raise godly children. While I'll still want my children to develop their abilities, I'll be equally concerned about their characters and their passion for God's work. Almost five hundred years ago, Martin Luther wrote, "But the greatest good in married life, that which makes all suffering and labor worthwhile, is that God grants offspring and commands that they be brought up to worship and serve him. In all the world this is the noblest and most precious work, because to God there can be nothing dearer than the salvation of souls."[2]

I'll be honest, I didn't know this when I first had kids. But whatever our initial reasons, what matters now is our *current* motivation. What is the grand scheme behind your family? What will motivate you to train and instruct your children instead of ignoring something because you're too tired, too distracted, or too fearful to address it? What greater end will fuel your efforts?

On one occasion in the New Testament a deeply troubled boy proved too difficult for the disciples to handle. His father appealed directly to Jesus, and Jesus said, with all his authority, "Bring the boy to me" (Mark 9:19).

That, in a nutshell, is what we are called to do as parents: bring the boy, bring the girl, to Jesus. Receive these tiny sinners into your home, by faith label them "Obadiah," and instruct them accordingly. Our highest good, our most reverent charge, is to make the most of every day in the hope that our son or daughter, whether he or she serves the king or cleans toilets, can be labeled a "servant of Yahweh."

Some children will follow eagerly; others will overwhelm us with their resistance. But our ultimate aim, our end goal, is this: "Bring the boy to [Jesus]."

May the prayer of our hearts be, "Lord, refine my motivations, purify my actions, and energize my heart so that I do all I can to help my children find their greatest joy and their highest aim in serving you."

*Heavenly Father, give us new hearts, new minds, and new perspective so that we can refocus on raising children who, first and foremost, will worship and serve you. Guide us as we seek to introduce them to who you are, and help us to find the best way to lead them to a sincere and true faith in Jesus Christ. In Jesus' name we pray, amen.*

## Questions for Reflection

1. Have you ever asked the question, "Why did we have children?" What do you think your primary motivation to have children was?

2. If someone were to examine your schedule, your conversations with your children, and your focus, would they say it seems that your highest goal is to help your children come to a saving faith in Jesus Christ and to offer themselves as servants of God's kingdom? If not, what do you need to alter in your lifestyle and focus?

# 6

## HIDING

*By faith Moses' parents hid him for three*
*months after he was born, because . . . they*
*were not afraid of the king's edict.*
Hebrews 11:23

By *faith* Moses' parents hid him from the wrath of Pharaoh. Normally, we think of hiding as cowardly, as an act of fear. But when it comes to our children, hiding them can be a tremendous act of brave faith.

The Bible tells us there is one who seeks our children's downfall every bit as much as Pharaoh sought the death of Moses: the devil, Satan (1 Peter 5:8). As spiritually attuned parents, it is our calling, our duty, and our responsibility to "hide" our children from this nemesis. In fact, Peter tells us to be "alert" to the devil's schemes. While some go overboard and focus on Satan too much, most of us moderns probably fall into the other extreme—failing to recognize his schemes or even acknowledge his existence.

Let me be blunt: Satan hates your children. He wants nothing more than to see them waste their lives, rebel against God, and cause untold heartache and pain during the short lives they spend on this earth. If he can't steal their salvation, at least he wants to keep them from becoming productive, reproducing members of God's church. The future of God's work on this earth depends on believing children who will speak up with courage, faith, and integrity. Where you see a baby, Satan sees a sworn enemy of his rebellion against God.

And yet, how often do we throw our children into Satan's path unprepared? We assume they'll absorb biblical teaching without any explicit effort on our part to ensure solid theological grounding. We give more thought to how they'll *get* to school than to who is teaching them (and what they are being taught). Since we don't guard their associations, we allow them to get together with whomever, whenever, wherever. We let them watch movies with horrendous messages, as long as there aren't "too many" bad words and its sexuality isn't "too explicit."

In fact, some would say that to even think about hiding our children is to give way to fear and to be overprotective (and maybe you thought just that when you read the opening paragraphs of this devotion)—but when Moses' parents hid him, the biblical writer recounts it as an act of *great faith*, not fear. Perhaps we've gone too far in the other direction, so fearful of oversheltering our children that we neglect the very real danger that full, unhindered exposure to this world can cause.

We hide our children in spiritually healthy ways by praying for them, by monitoring what and whom they see, and by warning them. The "hiding level" changes, of course, as they mature, but even when they get placed in harm's way, we must give them all they need to confront the enemy of their souls. I remember a recent conversation with my teenage son about pornography, now that he has access to the Internet. "Champ," I said, "pornography is sort of like smoking. Even if you stop smoking, your lungs will still bear the marks of that poison, because you get only one pair of lungs. The same is true of your mind.

If you fill up your brain with that stuff, God may forgive you, but you're impacting the only mind you'll ever have. Keep it pure. Keep it fresh. God has a reason for telling us to flee from sexual immorality of any kind."

Hiding isn't based in fear; it's based in faith. I wish I had the space to quote all of Psalm 91, but let's focus on just the first three verses (though I recommend you read the whole psalm later):

> Whoever who dwells in the shelter of the Most High
>     will rest in the shadow of the Almighty.
> I will say of the LORD, "He is my refuge and my fortress,
>     my God, in whom I trust."
> Surely he will save you
>     from the fowler's snare
>     and from the deadly pestilence.

We Christians are blessed with a hiding place refuge that is as beautiful and wondrous as it is secure: the shelter of the Most High, the shadow of the Almighty. We needn't live by fear; on the contrary, because of God's provision we live with the steady confidence that when we do our part, God will do his. For the time will surely come when we can no longer hide our children, when it's no longer appropriate to shelter them, when our children must face the world head-on, with all its temptations and traps.

It felt a bit unnerving for my wife and me to send our son off to public school after nine years of homeschooling, but we did our best to make sure he was prepared—including having him read a book I'm happy to recommend (*How to Stay Christian in High School* by Steve Gerali), engaging in a lot of conversation with him, and offering up a lot of prayers for him. The conversations continue—when issues come up, we spend time discussing them in light of God's Word. Even while unleashing him into the world, we seek to "hide" him in God's truth, wisdom, and revelation.

Parents, be vigilant. The world is *not* a safe place where children can wander unprotected and unwatched. Your child, born of Christian parents, has an implacable, anti-Christian enemy. But also be encouraged. When we hide our children in the shelter of the Most High, in the very shadow of the Almighty, we need not be afraid. We *must* be vigilant, but our alertness stems from the confidence we have in a mighty God who works with us to raise godly children for the sake of his kingdom.

Is your child in a dangerous place? Rescue him. Is your child unduly influenced by a harmful antagonist? Rescue her. Let's warn them of the enemy, but encourage them with the comfort and confidence of seeking refuge in the shadow and the shelter of the Almighty. By faith let's hide our children while we still can.

*Heavenly Father, guide us as we seek to protect our children. Help us to find that line of speaking up when appropriate and knowing when to let go. Be our light, our counselor, and our helper as we seek to protect and prepare our children for the life ahead. In Jesus' name, amen.*

## Questions for Reflection

1. Does thinking about "spiritual warfare" make you a little nervous when it comes to your children, or is this a familiar thought for you?
2. Discuss where each child may be most vulnerable to lies, and pray about how to point him or her to the truth.

# 7

# A SEASON OF SACRIFICE

*After all, children should not have to save
up for their parents, but parents for their
children. So I will very gladly spend for you
everything I have and expend myself as well.*

2 CORINTHIANS 12:14–15

IN MY BOOK *AUTHENTIC FAITH* I TALK ABOUT HOW GOD ONCE challenged my hesitancy with the words, "What you're really saying, Gary, is that you're willing to act like a Christian *so long as it doesn't cost you anything.*"

I've found the same principle at work in my parenting. I love many things about being a dad, but I sometimes have difficulty accepting the fact that parenting often *costs* me something. That's the principle Paul talks about in 2 Corinthians 12:14–15: "After all, children should not have to save up for their parents, but parents for their children. So I will very gladly spend for you everything I have and expend myself as well." Though Paul is discussing finances, the extension is obvious: parents should sacrifice on behalf of their children.

Judah, father of the tribe into which Jesus would be born, faced such a sacrifice in his own family life. As his family's food dwindled during a severe famine, Judah knew there was only one place where grain could be found: Egypt. But his brother Joseph, who controlled the grain in Egypt, had made it clear that no grain would be given unless Judah's father, Israel, allowed Benjamin—Joseph's brother—to come with them. Israel was terrified of losing Benjamin, so Judah made himself responsible for Benjamin's safety: "Send the boy along with me and we will go at once. . . . I myself will guarantee his safety; you can hold me personally responsible for him. If I do not bring him back to you and set him here before you, I will bear the blame before you all my life" (Genesis 43:8–9).

Judah wasn't the oldest son; why should he step up and make this offer? Even so, he was the only one willing to lay his own life on the line. His family's survival depended on it. Judah stepped up and said, "I will take responsibility for this child. I'll do whatever it takes to set him before you."

Judah's guarantee came at a steep cost. When Joseph framed Benjamin for stealing a silver cup, Judah offered himself as the substitute—and spent many months in jail—so that Benjamin could return safely to his father.

Judah's sacrifice foreshadowed Jesus' sacrifice and his guarantee of our safety. Just like Judah, Jesus stepped up and said, "I will make myself personally responsible, regardless of the cost to my own welfare."

Now we parents, spiritual descendants of Judah and Jesus, are called to step up and make the sacrifices for our own children. Just like Judah, we are to look at our heavenly Father and say, "I will do whatever it takes to set these children before you. I will make the sacrifice; I will be engaged in their lives; I will correct them, counsel them, encourage them, and pray for them. Regardless of the cost, I *will* set these children before you."

This calling gets tested every day. I've written before that I'm not much of a night person. I work a couple hours before breakfast. I work after breakfast. I work after lunch. By the time supper rolls around, I like to think of my day as "over." That's my time to relax, to take it easy, to read, maybe even to watch a little television.

That's the way I like it—except that with teenagers, the evening is now the best time of the day to meet with them, talk with them, and spend time with them. Am I willing to be a dad *as long as it doesn't cost me my evenings,* or am I willing to be a dad, regardless of the cost?

Every minute we spend with a son or daughter comes at the expense of something else we could be doing. Lisa and I have seen couples stop making these sacrifices. Their kids become chore machines and taxi customers, but the parents have decided that their kids will no longer "get in the way" of their hobbies.

Contrast this attitude with that of my friend Kevin DeVere. Kevin is a middle school principal, so he keeps fairly rigid hours. Like me, Kevin has embarked on a middle-age journey of running marathons— and the longer training runs can take three hours or more. On our drive to a half marathon, I lamented to Kevin about quitting work early to get the training runs in before dark. Then I asked Kevin what he did, given that he had a much less flexible schedule.

"I'm kind of embarrassed to say," he said.

"Tell me," I urged him.

"Well, when I need to run long, I get up at 3:20 a.m."

"You've got to be kidding me!" I said. "So it's dark the entire time you're running?"

"Yeah, but Gary, how can I come home from work at 5:00 p.m. and tell my kids, 'Sorry, guys, but Daddy has to leave for another two hours'? There's no way I can do that."

Kevin is an example of a man who fits his hobby around his family rather than the other way around.

In fact, parenting may be best defined as *a season of sacrifice*. It ends when the children mature—but not one day before. To stop sacrificing in the middle of our kids' adolescence is the spiritual equivalent of deserting an army in the middle of battle.

I know it gets tiring, and it's not easy. But we have to finish this work. Our kids, by their existence, make a legitimate spiritual claim on our time, our money, and our focus. They necessarily limit what we may appropriately do outside the home. Let's avoid falling into the trap God has pointed out in my own life: "What you're really saying is that you're willing to act like a parent *as long as it doesn't cost you anything.*"

Finish this season of sacrifice.

*Heavenly Father, give us willing hearts to accept this season of sacrifice.*
*Let our attitude be one of joy, not frustration, so that our children feel*
*as if they are blessings instead of burdens. In Jesus' name, amen.*

## Questions for Reflection

1. What sacrifice is parenting calling you to endure right now?
2. How can you encourage each other to embrace such sacrifices while still maintaining a positive, joyful attitude?

# 8

# WHAT MATTERS MOST

*Martha was distracted by all the*
*preparations that had to be made....*
*"Martha, Martha," the Lord answered, "you are*
*worried and upset about many things, but few things*
*are needed—or indeed only one. Mary has chosen what*
*is better, and it will not be taken away from her."*
LUKE 10:40–42

MATT CAME HOME ONE AFTERNOON AND PAUSED ON HIS WAY into the house when he saw a long, white scratch down the side of his one-week-old minivan.

"What happened?" he bellowed.

His daughter confessed that she had ridden her bike into the garage and scraped the brand-new vehicle with her handlebars. Matt got a bit heated, because his daughter had broken an ironclad rule and cost him a lot of money and hassle in the process.

Laura, Matt's wife, came out when she heard the "conversation" and immediately took their daughter away, saying just three words: "It's a *car*."

Those three short syllables were enough to chasten my friend.

"My daughter had scratched metal," Matt admitted, "but I crushed a person."

Matt's insight—comparing scratched metal to a crushed person—helps me keep perspective. What really matters more? It's impossible for any kid to live in a house without occasionally making a mess, breaking something, or leaving a permanent mark behind. Yet it's so easy to make them feel guilty for inconveniencing us. It's also easy to forget what matters most—scratched metal, or a crushed person.

During his induction ceremony into the Baseball Hall of Fame, Harmon Killebrew spoke fondly of his parents. He recounted how one day he and his brother were out playing in the yard, and their mother got upset. "You're tearing up the grass!" she complained.

To which Harmon's dad replied, "We're not raising grass, we're raising boys."

When our kids are young, life resembles a blur. We try to keep the house relatively clean, struggle to balance competing demands, work to keep passion and romance in our marriages, and, I hope, seek first the kingdom of God. In the midst of this blur, secondary aims—a clean house, a postcard-perfect yard, and so on—can become enemies of our ultimate purpose.

I'm not saying that a clean house doesn't matter or that a yard shouldn't be treated appropriately, but I think Harmon's dad was on to something. In the end, what matters more? Life today demands—even ensures—that some *good* aims will have to get temporarily shelved in order for us to fulfill the *ultimate* aim. In the twilight of these choices, we determine what matters most.

Let's be careful we don't value a spotless floor over a positive, nurturing, and encouraging relationship with our kids; that we don't make them feel guilty for the impossibility of living in a house without leaving some kind of mess behind. The day will come when they won't soil the floor, touch the walls, or create additional laundry—and I suspect we'll miss the good old days when the yard showed the effects of heavy traffic and the house revealed the presence of children.

But maybe you need to deliver *yourself*, not your children, from these expectations. I recently walked into the master bedroom after being away, and my wife apologized for the mess. In the previous twenty-four hours, my wife had worked as hard as any woman in this nation. I knew her schedule; I knew the choices she had made. And *every choice was the right one*. Something *had* to give. She had nothing to apologize for.

Set yourself—and your family—free. Except for those who can afford outside help, few of us with kids still around will ever qualify for a *Better Homes and Gardens* spread. Our lawns may not get gawked at by visitors or passersby. There may exist blatant evidence of a few projects that still need to be done. But we're not raising grass; we're raising kids.

Let's remember Matt's insight: scratched metal doesn't justify crushing persons.

*Heavenly Father, help us to maintain the attitude that people, especially our children, matter most. Make our homes bastions of laughter, joy, and acceptance, not pressure-filled places where one footprint or fingerprint elicits howls of wrath. In Jesus' name, amen.*

## Questions for Reflection

1. Have you recently valued "things" over children's feelings and perhaps wounded one of your children? Do you need to go to that child and say "I'm sorry"?
2. Are you keeping the right balance between viewing your house as a home instead of a museum, or a practice field instead of a showroom?

# THE SONG OF THE
# CHILDLESS WOMAN

*He raises the poor from the dust*
*and lifts the needy from the ash heap;*
*he seats them with princes,*
*with the princes of his people.*
*He settles the childless woman in her home*
*as a happy mother of children.*

PSALM 113:7–9

IN HIS NOVEL *HARVARD YARD*, WILLIAM MARTIN DESCRIBES A prosperous seventeenth-century Puritan who faces one of life's greatest poverties: childlessness.

> John needed only to look out his window to see the Lord's bounty upon him. He could gaze across his vegetable garden and down to the Great Cove, to his ships—half a dozen by his wife's inheritance, half a dozen his by his own intelligence. . . . But his piety and faith had not been great enough, because the richest of the Lord's blessings—a house filled with happy noise—had not come to John Wedge. His morning sounds were always the same—the humming of the slave woman who

stirred his porridge, the whisk of a broom worked by an indentured servant, and the quiet coughing of his wife. He heard no childish bickering, no mothering voice rising to calm a dispute, and for those, he would have surrendered everything else.[1]

It's not often I'm compelled to stop when reading a novel, but I certainly did with this last powerful turn of phrase: *and for those, he would have surrendered everything else.* Parenting is a lot of very hard and very tiring work. In the midst of the grind, we can forget the song of the barren couple that opens up for us entirely new horizons of insight and thanksgiving.

In reality, we're living a dream.

One of the greatest blessings God can give is to take a childless couple and make them, as the psalmist wrote, "happy [parents] of children." Kids are a tremendous blessing—flesh-covered miracles of God's gracious favor. But sometimes, when we get too close to the work, when we lose so much sleep, we become blind to children as blessings and see them only as burdens.

But where we see dirty diapers, the barren couple sees a living, breathing baby they get to clean.

Where our culture views as a "prisoner" a parent who quits his or her job to stay home, the barren couple sees a home filled with laughter and the delight of their precious child's presence.

Where we see financial obligation, the barren couple sees something finally worth spending their money on.

The next time you're tempted to complain about all those car trips to shuttle kids around, don't forget this: a barren woman would gladly drive twenty-four hours straight if only she had a child to transport.

May we never lose sight of the true miracle: God has placed a living, breathing human being into our care!

When I wrote the first draft of *Sacred Parenting,* some early readers challenged me when I wrote that there was no joy like a family's joy. Some asked me whether this statement might offend singles.

The last thing I want to do is offend singles, but I stand behind what I said: there really *is* no joy like a family's joy. Certainly, singles can still have a rich, meaningful, and fulfilled life. They may well experience certain edges of carefree happiness married people will never know. But they will never experience the singular phenomenon of laughing with your child on the long journey we call parenting. When that laughter is born out of living together twenty-four hours a day, caring for them and sacrificing for them and delighting in them and disciplining them and getting angry at them and having them break your heart, melt your heart, and enlarge your heart—well, there really is nothing else like it.

There just isn't.

The psalmist couldn't have been clearer: one of God's richest blessings is to establish the barren woman in her home as a *happy* mother of children.

If God has placed you in your home as a happy mother (or father) of children, accept this as God's good favor. Thank him zealously, and often, for this journey you are on. Do you see your children as a blessing? Do you realize how some barren women would give their right arms to have what you have? They would gladly take all your troubles without complaining—if their empty arms could be filled with even *one* child, let alone two, or three, or four.

Last night I drove my children home from youth group. As the kids and I talked, laughed, and shared stories in our own car, I thought, *There is nowhere else on earth I'd rather be than right here. There is no one else I'd rather be with than these children. For this one moment, everything is just as it should be. It's perfect, and I'm content.*

No, none of us have perfect children. Sometimes, we don't even have pleasant children! But whenever we're tempted to complain, let's consider the ache of the childless couple.

*Heavenly Father, thank you for the blessing of children, whether they have joined our family through biological birth or adoption. Help us to remember how much we desired these children, and grant us the grace to never take them for granted, and to never let the blessing be overshadowed by the burden of caring for them and providing for them. In Jesus' name, amen.*

## Questions for Reflection

1. Talk about what you would have missed if you didn't have one or more of your children. How has each one brought his or her own unique blessings into your family?

2. Discuss how you can turn the "burdens" of parenting into "blessings" when you choose to look at them from a different perspective.

# FEAR FACTOR

*A furious squall came up, and the waves broke*
*over the boat, so that it was nearly swamped.*
*Jesus was in the stern, sleeping on a cushion.*

MARK 4:37–38

FRIENDS OF OURS HAD TWO CHILDREN IN COLUMBINE HIGH School during the terrible shooting attack of April 1999. Several other tragic events—largely unreported nationally—assaulted the city over the ensuing months. On top of all this, a disturbed church member started violently harassing my friends' family (both are on staff at a local church) by throwing manure on their car, writing filthy graffiti on their church office windows, slashing their tires, and once even bashing in their car windows outside their home.

All the tragic events happening in the city, combined with the personal war waged against the family, led my friends' young daughter to say, "I can't take this anymore." They somewhat reluctantly agreed to send their daughter to an out-of-state boarding school. After months of research, they chose a highly respected private institution located in Long Island, New York.

My friends dropped off this psychologically shaken girl in New

York on September 9, 2001. Forty-eight hours later, terrorists crashed two planes into the World Trade Center.

Most of our children will never face such a traumatic series of events, but even for those of us who live in anonymous towns and face normal, coming-of-age challenges, fear for our children is an occupational hazard, because the dangers are very real.

The great Baptist preacher Charles Spurgeon addressed this in one of his sermons. You'll recall that Jesus once fell asleep during a storm so fierce that his disciples feared for their lives. We know Jesus cared enough for his disciples to die for them, yet in this moment of crisis his calm attitude was so steady it almost tempts us to believe he didn't care—or to conclude he lived with an absolute trust many of us lack. Spurgeon deftly compared Jesus' calm demeanor to our fretful worrying: "We do not have half the confidence in God that we ought to have—not even the best of us. The Lord deserves our limitless belief, our unquestioning confidence, our undisturbed reliance."[1]

Can any of us suggest that God *isn't* worthy of "our limitless belief, our unquestioning confidence," even "our undisturbed reliance"? And yet, how often do we fret, as though his providential care simply can't be counted on with regard to something as precious as our children?

Just as Jesus put all his confidence in his Father, so, Spurgeon said, we should put our confidence in the same heavenly Father:

> If a watchman were hired to guard my house, I would be foolish if I also sat up for fear of thieves. Why have a watchman if I cannot trust him to watch? "Cast thy burden upon the LORD" (Psalm 55:22 KJV), but when you have done so, leave it with the Lord and do not try to carry it yourself. Otherwise, you mock God; you use the name of God, but not the reality of God. Lay down every care, even as Jesus did when

He went calmly to the rear part of the ship, quietly took a pillow, and went to sleep.[2]

Jesus' confidence in the heavenly Father gave him a fierce freedom that could stare down any storm, because Jesus never compared the storm to those under his care; on the contrary, he compared the storm to the God who rules the weather. He wasn't careless about his disciples' welfare; he simply felt certain of his Father's providential involvement, concern, and sovereign protection.

I'm perhaps most convicted by Spurgeon's charge that we *use the name of God, but not the reality of God*. Sometimes when I fret, I find myself acting like a functional atheist, claiming belief while stubbornly refusing to exercise—or at least rest in—faith. Perhaps God gave us children in part to make our own faith more real, to keep us from settling for merely naming God rather than pushing into the reality of God.

Spurgeon freely admits that caring for children, more than anything else in human experience, has a way of pushing fear into our hearts:

> You feel that you cannot cast upon God your burden of concern about your children. But your Lord trusted the Father with those dear to Him. Do you not think that Christ's disciples were as precious to Him as our children are to us? . . . Our Lord regarded with intense affection those whom He had chosen and called, and who had been with Him in His temptation. Even so, He was quite content to leave them all in the care of His Father and go to sleep.[3]

How can we argue with this? Do we really want to suggest that Jesus acted negligently with his disciples, or that he didn't truly care for them? He knew he was sending them into a dangerous and theoretically fatal encounter—but he also knew the encounter would be governed by the providence of God and filtered through his loving care, not determined by chance. Some of us parents insult God by verbally placing our children under his protection but then worrying as though he were either deaf or powerless. Spurgeon gently encourages us, "No horrible turn of events has ever occurred in a matter that I have left in God's care."[4]

Much of our fretting is simply a lack of faith. We have a God; why worry as though we don't? This week, let's begin the journey of confident reliance on God by asking ourselves some rhetorical questions that will cement this truth to our souls:

- Who cares more about our children—us, or God?
- Who is better able and more equipped to protect our children—us, or God?
- Who looks on our children with greater understanding of the future—not just in ten years' time but for all eternity?
- Who has the power to make all things turn out for the good for those who love him and have been called according to his purpose?

Let your children make God's care and providence ever more real to you. May we one day be like Jesus, whose great confidence in the heavenly Father enabled him, even in the midst of a storm, to quietly fall asleep in all peace, entrusting those he loved to the care of his Father who never sleeps.

*Heavenly Father, we thank you that while you rule the heavens and the earth you are intimately watchful over every one of your children. We place our kids in your care. Give us the faith to leave them there. In Jesus' name, amen.*

## Questions for Reflection

1. In what area is it hardest for you to trust God with your children?
2. How might God help our kids grow as they confront frightening realities?
3. How can we *leave* our children in God's care after we *place* them there? What spiritual practices can we adopt that will help us to worry less and trust God more?

# RUDE IS RUDE

*"See that you do not despise one of these little ones. For I tell you that their angels in heaven always see the face of my Father in heaven."*
MATTHEW 18:10

JESUS TELLS US THAT THE HEAVENLY FATHER NEVER MISSES what happens to one of his "little ones," so we can feel certain he sees everything going on behind our walls.

Is that an encouragement, or a warning?

We need to remember that a smaller person is not "less" of a person; a younger person is not less valuable than an older person—but why as parents do we sometimes take liberties with our children that we would never take with anyone else?

Miss Manners' take on this is as right as it is blunt:

Rudeness to children counts as rudeness. The fact that people are smaller and blood relatives does not mean that it is open season on insulting them. Besides, it teaches them the technique and thus leads to such tedious exchanges as, "Don't you dare talk to Mommy like that," "But that's what you said to me," "That's different," "Why is it different?" and so on. What makes it different is that when children do it, parents call it "sassing," and when parents do it, parents call it discipline.[1]

Parents who are rude to their children have forgotten that their children belong first to *God*. These are not *our* children to do with as we please; they were made by God, and he has designed a unique future for each one of them. If we complicate that future by belittling them and tearing them down instead of building them up, we work against God's purposes—and we can be sure he will call us to account.

We're not raising crops, nor are we caring for pet hamsters. As parents, we are called to shape and influence living human beings—made in the image of God—for whom Jesus Christ died. Our actions can have severe consequences, and we have the power to shatter these fragile beings. Some parents inflict this damage subtly, perhaps by a constant barrage of perfectionistic banter that guarantees their kids feel like they never measure up. Maybe we wound them in a passive-aggressive way, maliciously withholding the affection we know they crave, with the result that they slip into a life of promiscuity. Maybe we get too busy and by our neglect fail to train them adequately, with the result that they make poor financial or life choices and end up ruined.

Whatever our failing, the stakes couldn't be higher—for us and our kids. A parent's malicious act of neglect can devastate the child as much as it spiritually ruins the parent, for to become our children's enemy is to become *God's* enemy. Jesus warns us, "If anyone causes one of these little ones—those who believe in me—to stumble, it would be better for them to have a large millstone hung around their neck and to be drowned in the depths of the sea" (Matthew 18:6).

"Well," some might say, "what if my child makes himself *my* enemy?" Even so, how does Jesus tell us to treat our enemies? To be rude to them? To belittle them, shame them, and make them feel small? No! Jesus says, "Love your enemies" (Matthew 5:44).

God feels so passionate about our children's well-being that he did not spare even his own Son in his desire to secure their eternal destiny. Will a God who offered the supreme sacrifice, who paid the highest cost imaginable, fail to even *notice* the rude ways we respond to our children? Will a heavenly Father so engaged in their spiritual health forget to watch what is going on in our "private" homes?

According to the Bible, there is no such thing as a private home. Children have spiritual beings charged specifically with watching over their welfare: "See that you do not despise one of these little ones. For I tell you that their angels in heaven always see the face of my Father in heaven" (Matthew 18:10). To invite a child into your home is to guarantee divine presence and notice. Perhaps the presence of children can remind us that we don't live in secret; we live in full view of an active God who judges our actions.

God cares. God watches.

This week, remind yourself that God hears every conversation and sees every act. We said it before, but let's say it again: *God is in the room*.

*Heavenly Father, now that we know "rude is rude," regardless of how old someone is, give us a new respect, gentleness, and patience for each one of our children. Help us to correct them in a way that honors you as an ever-present Father. In Jesus' name, amen.*

## Questions for Reflection

1. Why do you think it feels so easy to be rude to our kids and to speak to them in a way we'd never speak to an adult? What can we do to change this?

2. How can the spiritual truth that God and his angels are ever present in our homes, watching over our children's welfare, transform the way we speak to them and treat them?

# 12

# "IT WAS LIKE HE NEVER EXISTED"

*What do people gain from all their labors*
*at which they toil under the sun?*
ECCLESIASTES 1:3

"IT WAS LIKE HE NEVER EXISTED."

I looked at Ernie as he spoke these words and saw the gentle grace of a life well lived. He had worked hard to support his family, and now in retirement he was pouring his energies into building up the men's ministry of his church.

Ernie chose early retirement in part because of something that occurred just a few years before he left. He worked for one of the most stable and famous companies in the United States. Until the late 1980s, if you could land a job with this company, you pretty much figured you had a job for life. They paid well but demanded a lot out of their workers.

"We gave our lives to the company," Ernie said. "They took care of us, but they expected us to organize our lives around our work. If we ever said no, even once, we'd be taken off the track of promotion and kept in a vocational eddy for the rest of our careers. So we got to work early and stayed late."

One of Ernie's coworkers was a younger man in his late forties who had worked side by side with Ernie for years. One morning, the man failed to arrive at work, and Ernie assumed he was sick—until a call came from his wife at 8:30 a.m. with the shocking news that the man had died. His heart had stopped while he was eating breakfast.

"They chose his replacement that afternoon," Ernie said, "and the man was on the job early the next morning—less than twenty-four hours after his predecessor was pronounced dead. We spent about fifteen minutes giving the new guy a quick orientation, but he was familiar with what we were doing so it didn't take much. Everything ran incredibly smoothly."

Ernie paused, gazing out the windshield, before he went on. "None of the other coworkers went to the guy's funeral. They knew the guy but didn't know his family, so they figured it didn't matter much. After he was buried, as far as the company was concerned, it was like he never existed. He gave his entire life to the company, coming in early and working late, but the company didn't miss a step—not a single step— once he died. It's terrible to say this, but in a way, the company was less inconvenienced by his death than if he had taken a two-week vacation."

Ernie took me back to my hotel after a speaking engagement and dropped me off, but his words remained with me.

The next day, I walked in the front door of my home, heard the familiar cry, "Papa!" and soon felt three pairs of arms around my legs and waist. We went for a walk, and Graham, who was then just four years old, held my wife's hand and mine at the same time, proudly proclaiming, "Now the whole family is together!" He kissed Lisa's hand and then kissed mine.

Kelsey, then just two, got a big smile on her face when she looked back at me and called out, "Papa's home!"

Ernie's words, "It was like he never existed," hovered over me. I believe they may have been a significant factor in my decision to become self-employed.

I had that talk with Ernie more than fifteen years ago; I don't even know if he's still alive. But his insight will remain with me for the rest of my life. Many people clamor for our attention, but only a very few make room for us in their hearts. To some our absence amounts to a mere inconvenience; to others it feels like a devastating spiritual, emotional, and relational black hole.

Which group will get our best thoughts, our most earnest energy, and the most productive hours of our lives? I guess it comes down to this: Whom do I really want to disappoint with my no? The kids whose faces light up when they see me? The wife who will be there for me, whether I'm making megabucks, retired, or unemployed? Or a business that views me as an efficient useful cog that meets its needs at the moment, while seeing me as utterly replaceable?

I'm not antibusiness—not by any means. God uses businesses, large and small, to feed many families. But the truth is, we matter more than we may realize to our families and probably less than we'd like to admit to our employer.

Let's reward those whose affection is genuine and sincere.

*Heavenly Father, help us to learn from the examples of others and from Ecclesiastes 1:3 to prioritize relationships and family in regard to where we put our best efforts and focus. Help us to so order our days that the people who are most affected by our passing will also be the ones who received the bulk of our attention. In Jesus' name, amen.*

## Questions for Reflection

1. How is this teaching true even if you don't always feel appreciated at home?

2. Talk about how well both of you are balancing vocation and family life.

# 13

# A PARENT TO BE PROUD OF

*Parents are the pride of their children.*
PROVERBS 17:6

AS A YOUNG BOY, I FELT GREAT JOY GROWING UP WITH A FATHER I could look up to. My dad worked in management at a public utility, and he regularly helped some of our friends get summer jobs there. When a girlfriend of mine got hired, everybody kept asking her if she had met "the big man" yet—they were referring not to his size but to the fact that he ran the whole office.

"No," she replied, "I don't think so."

"You will," they told her, "but don't worry. He's a really nice guy."

When the time came for the grand introduction, my girlfriend laughed as she realized she *had* met "the big man"—and my dad gave her a hug. When she told me about this, I can't tell you how much my heart swelled that others looked up to my dad like I did. I knew my dad wouldn't scandalize our family. He had a respectable job, and he was a man of character and integrity. I felt proud to be his son.

Part of the discipline of parenthood is to be a person my children can feel proud of. *My* reputation will affect *theirs*; I don't want them to have to feel embarrassed to "admit" that, yes, they're related to me. I've invited a few key people to keep me accountable for this very reason. I don't want to do anything that would make my kids ashamed. And since I know the heart is deceitful, I want other men to warn me when I'm getting too close to the boundaries.

Luke tells us that Elizabeth, the mother of John the Baptist, attracted God's attention in part because she was "righteous in the sight of God." She observed "all the Lord's commands and decrees blamelessly" (Luke 1:6). Like Elizabeth, we must consecrate ourselves for the purpose of raising one of God's image bearers. Andrew Murray reflects, "Every expectant mother should offer her body as the temple of the Holy Spirit, so that the very beginning of life in her may be overshadowed by the Holy Spirit."[1]

This consecration is an ongoing process. In fact, it's a very healthy exercise as a mother or father to ask, "What would my son or daughter think if they knew I was doing this?" There are many reasons to pursue holiness, but raising children is certainly one of the more important ones. So often, we parents become so consumed with our kids "staying out of trouble" that we forget *we* can get in just as much trouble. All of us—young and old alike—are called to offer our bodies as temples of the Holy Spirit.

Kids desire parents they can be proud of—even in the most extreme situations. While in a Communist prison because of his Christian beliefs, a father named Florescu was tortured with red-hot iron pokers and knives. When the torture didn't break Florescu's spirit, the Communists put starving rats into his cell through a long pipe, which meant Florescu could never get any sleep. As soon as he started to nod off, he'd literally get eaten, so he had to stay awake to defend himself. This went on for fourteen days, but still Florescu refused to reveal the names of other Christians in his fellowship.

Then the Communists brought in Florescu's fourteen-year-old son and whipped the boy in front of his father. As the young boy cried out, the Communists taunted Florescu, telling him they would continue to beat his son until he told them what they wanted to know.

Finally, Florescu had had enough. "Alexander!" he cried out. "I must say what they want. I can't bear your beating anymore!"

Astonishingly, young Alexander answered with an even more impassioned plea: "Father, don't do me the injustice of having a traitor as a parent. Withstand! If they kill me, I will die with the words, 'Jesus and my fatherland.'"[2]

Florescu never forgot his son's words: "Father, don't do me the injustice of having a traitor as a parent." For Florescu's son, having a father he could feel proud of was even more important than his own life. Maybe that's why Joshua's famous line, "As for me and my household, we will serve the LORD" (Joshua 24:15), begins with *me*. Before my household serves God, I commit myself to serving God. "As for *me* and my household . . ."

I don't want a traitor for a son, but, even more, my son doesn't want a traitor for a father.

*Heavenly Father, you are a God we are honored and proud to worship.*
*Help us to be parents our children can respect and admire. Win the*
*battle for our hearts and minds so that we can live as positive examples*
*for the children you've placed in our care. In Jesus' name, amen.*

## Questions for Reflection

1. This devotion calls us to a life inventory. Are you living in such a way that you can say to your kids what Paul said to the Corinthians: "Follow my example, as I follow the example of Christ" (1 Corinthians 11:1)?

2. Let's not just think negatively. What are we doing positively that will make our children proud? Do they ever see us acting with courage, conviction, and sacrifice?

# 14

# CUT DOWN

*In your relationships with one another, have*
*the same mindset as Christ Jesus:*
*Who, being in very nature God,*
*did not consider equality with God something*
*to be used to his own advantage;*
*rather, he made himself nothing*
*by taking the very nature of a servant,*
*being made in human likeness.*
*And being found in appearance as a man,*
*he humbled himself*
*by becoming obedient to death—*
*even death on a cross!*

PHILIPPIANS 2:5–8

CHRIST'S HUMBLING CONDESCENSION TO LEAVE THE GLORY OF heaven; set aside his majestic, unveiled deity; and become a breathing, bleeding, "bodyfied" man—a process known to theologians as the *kenosis*—provides a model for our own call to practice humility. By God's marvelous design, few life experiences humble us quite as effectively as parenting. As parents, we exchange our formerly spotless houses, ironed clothes, and ordered lives for the chaos of an incontinent, noisy, spit-producing being with a temper that needs to be tamed and with a piercing cry that rivals the sharpest fingernails ever scraped across a chalkboard.

This tiny tyrant is providentially placed into our house as part of a grand program: to mold his or her parents into the image of our Lord.

Writer Rachel Cusk recounts one of the most embarrassing moments of her life. She had met a friend for lunch at an outside table when the weather changed, and social disaster struck along with it:

> It starts to rain, hard. I try to pack the baby back into her pouch, and I do it clumsily and unconfidently, and suddenly she starts to cry, to scream with an extraordinary, primitive anguish; and I am in disarray, knocking over coffee cups, fumbling with change, trying to speak, to pacify, to explain, holding the baby this way and that in the drenching rain and finally running through the park, the empty pouch flapping at my front, the roaring baby held out before me like something on fire, my friend trotting embarrassed behind, until we reach the road and madly, desperately, I flag down a taxi and somehow force the chaos of us into it. "I'll call you soon," says my friend strangely. I glimpse her through the window, slim and well dressed, compact, somehow extraordinarily demanding and utterly implacable, politely waving from the pavement.[1]

The humbling part of parenting is that it puts us in positions where we will feel out of style, out of wits, and out of control—even though we may be well accomplished in other areas. George is a gym teacher who makes his living handling unruly kids. But even he confesses, "At work I got sixty strapping adolescents to jump when I blew a whistle. Then I came home and I couldn't get a twelve-pound infant to stop crying."[2] A Navy SEAL from Bellingham, Washington, said that "being a SEAL, that's easy. Try getting three young daughters to brush their teeth at the same time." He might feel very confident facing three trained terrorists in the dark, but those little girls are more than he can handle!

While some married couples avoid having children for precisely this reason—fearing the chaos, the mess, and the lack of control inherent in raising a tiny being born with a free will—others see the humbling process of parenting as one of its most precious purposes. Since, as believers, we are called by God to become like Christ, we welcome any relationship that reinforces this process. Orthodox theologian Paul Evdokimov made this observation:

> Motherhood is a special form of the feminine *kenosis* (emptying). The mother gives herself to the child, dies in part for it, follows the love of God that humbles itself, and in a certain sense repeats the utterance of John the Baptist, "He must grow greater, I must grow smaller." The sacrifice of the mother includes the sword of which Simeon speaks. In this sacrifice, every mother bends over the crucified Christ.[3]

What a line! *In this sacrifice, every mother bends over the crucified Christ.* This baby may redistribute your makeup, wreak havoc on your schedule, obliterate more than one mealtime, declare holy war on your wardrobe, end up canceling at least 50 percent of your social engagements, and grab a few fistfuls of hair while she's at it—but she will also set you free from the smug and arrogant self-centeredness that so many young adults without kids are known for. She will bid you to bend over the crucified Christ.

From a spiritual perspective—in the eyes of those who truly desire to experience Christ and who even aspire to become more like him—parenting is a brilliant spiritual pathway to growth and maturity in the Lord.

Kids are a clever package to accomplish such an aim, for we adults usually feel much too proud to choose a specific act we know will humble us. But the beauty of a baby, the emotional bond we build with them, and the miracle of cocreating a human life is intriguing enough that most of us are willing to give it a go, even knowing (in theory) that such a step will open the door to many humbling events.

Yes, you've felt embarrassed. Your "look" isn't what it used to be. You're no longer so confident when you go out in public.

Thank God. He is doing a marvelous work in your soul. While we might feel *momentarily* cut down as we sacrifice for our children, internally and eternally we are being strengthened, built up, and matured in all the right ways.

*Heavenly Father, give us the spirit of your humble Son, who so willingly condescended on our behalf. Let us embrace the embarrassing moments of being a parent, knowing that the difficult process is being used by you to refine our souls. Amen.*

## Questions for Reflection

1. Talk about how being a parent has humbled you and why that has been a good thing.
2. How can the humbling moments of parenting draw you ever closer to Jesus and even increase your understanding of him?

# 15

# THEY JUST DON'T
# UNDERSTAND

*Blessed are you when people insult you,*
*persecute you and falsely say all kinds*
*of evil against you because of me.*
MATTHEW 5:11

MELISSA HAS TO LEAVE HER HOME EVERY TUESDAY AND FRIDAY at 3:00 p.m. to take Christy to a physical therapy session on the other side of Chicago. Because she wants to leave Christy in school for as long as possible, the late-afternoon trips put them in the thick of commuter traffic, and they don't return home until 7:00 p.m.

Christy hates these therapy sessions, but they're doing wonders for her ability to walk with a normal gait. As Melissa welcomed Christy into the car one Tuesday afternoon, Christy hissed at her: "I'll never forgive you for doing this to me."

Melissa wanted to ask Christy what she wouldn't forgive: the four-hour trips twice a week through heavy traffic, all to help Christy walk better? The vacations she and her husband, Greg, had given up so they could have the roughly $1,200 a month to spend on special services, education, and therapies to help Christy learn how to cope? The many nights Melissa spent on the Internet, trying to find the best services and support materials to help Christy overcome her challenges? Melissa has given just about every ounce of strength she has to help Christy deal with her disabilities—and for *that*, Christy will never forgive her?

It's one thing to sacrifice for your child; it's another thing to have that child look at your sacrifice and act as though it were child abuse— but Melissa already felt tired. The other kids didn't feel well that day, so she had done some of their chores. She was afraid to speak a word, because she knew that once she started, she might never be able to stop. And who knows what she would say if her mouth ran on?

To be a parent is to be misunderstood. To be a mom or dad is to have your kids, extended family members, friends, and even strangers second-guess you, question your motives, and pass judgment on your decisions. And to have our good motives questioned is certainly one of the most frustrating human experiences we face.

But would you like to know the secret blessing behind this pain? Every effective Christian worker will eventually be misunderstood, at least on occasion. When God allows us to confront this process as parents, he is preparing us to handle a fact of life with regard to working on behalf of his kingdom: *to minister is to be attacked, questioned, and maligned.*

In fact, during the time Jesus walked this earth, he was almost universally misunderstood. At times, even Jesus' own family considered him crazy (Mark 3:20–21). The religious leaders misunderstood Jesus' ministry, accusing him of being in league with the devil (Mark 3:22). Civic authorities thought Jesus' actions made absolutely no sense (Matthew 27:12–14). Even Jesus' own disciples had trouble understanding him (Mark 8:31–33).

Jesus came to us as God and was accused of being the devil. He spoke the truth and yet was called a liar. He willingly went to the cross out of obedience to his Father and yet was labeled a blasphemer. He embodied our only hope, yet died as a criminal. If anybody was continually misunderstood, it was Jesus. No one's intentions, abilities, and motives got distorted and challenged more often than Jesus'.

When God allows others to think less of you, to judge you, to challenge you, to malign you, he is bringing you into rare but intimate country—the sufferings of Christ. This is where the valley of misunderstanding stretches far and wide and where seemingly few places of rest exist. Though you've no doubt wanted to leave this valley many times, God's severe mercy keeps you there. You get to experience a side of him that others will never know. And God may be preparing you for a ministry somewhere down the road that will bring additional misunderstandings.

I want Christ's power. I want Christ's love. I want Christ's wisdom. Who doesn't? But Paul invites us into an even more intimate relationship—Christ's sufferings: "I want to know Christ—yes, to know the power of his resurrection and *participation in his sufferings*" (Philippians 3:10, emphasis added). A child who brings multiple misunderstandings may be your surest passport to that holy place.

This week, reflect on how difficult it is to do what you know must be done with your children, even though others (including your children) question your motives. Ask God to strengthen you to live in accordance with his will, not for the world's pleasure or applause. Seek to become a spiritually stronger parent who, when freed from the need to be understood, appreciated, or affirmed, can join Jesus Christ in preaching a message the world has never thought made much sense.

*Lord Jesus, how it must have grieved your soul to act solely out of love and to be accused of hate. Draw us close to you and give us your strength when we seek to do what is best for our children yet are questioned, maligned, and resented. Help us always act with pure motives. In your name we pray, amen.*

## Questions for Reflection

1. Have you ever experienced a moment like Melissa—doing something out of love and having a child turn it around into a form of punishment? How did it make you feel? How did you cope with it?

2. Why do you think it's so important—not just as a parent, but as a called servant in God's kingdom—to learn how to do what is right and loving even when others say we are doing the wrong thing out of hate?

# 16

# I'VE HAD MY TURN

*"Can a mother forget the baby at her breast*
*and have no compassion on the child she has borne?*
*Though she may forget,*
*I will not forget you!*
*See, I have engraved you on the palms of my hands."*

ISAIAH 49:15–16

KELSEY AND I WERE ENJOYING BREAKFAST AT KELSEY'S favorite restaurant—the International House of Pancakes. Celebrating her eleventh birthday, Kelsey felt in a bit of a panic because her beloved "Funny Face Pancakes" are served only to customers twelve and under; she had just fifty-two weeks left to enjoy those chocolate chip confections passed off as a breakfast. Three elderly men, whom we see almost every time we visit, sat behind us. If these men aren't in their eighties, they must be in their nineties, and they have to be just about the most pleasant group of men I've ever seen. The waitresses all get a hug, and every diner receives a hearty hello for a greeting—and they clearly have a deep affection for one another. One man held the arm of the other as he shuffled into the booth.

As is common with people with less-than-sharp hearing, they speak loudly. "Loud," in fact, understates the case. One of these men has a voice roughly equal to a foghorn. "Gimme one of those senior breakfasts," he called out to a waitress a good fifteen feet away—but you could've heard him across the freeway.

"Just one?"

"No, wait. Joe's coming. Better make that two. Bill, he likes something else."

Kelsey smiled, leaned in close to me, and whispered, "Daddy?"

"Yeah, honey?"

"When you get to be that old, I'm going to do the ordering for you."

I can't tell you how thrilled I was to hear Kelsey talk about going to IHOP with me when I'm in my eighties. Right now, I go there for her. The food doesn't do much for me, but Kelsey loves it. I can certainly imagine a time, however, when that dynamic will flip-flop, and Kelsey will pick me up to make sure I get out of the house.

Looking forward to this long-term relationship with my child made me all the more sad to read of a woman who rarely sees her children or grandchildren. Instead, she spends all her time caring for her pets. Her daughter keeps trying to get Grandma to visit, but "Betty Jean tells her the same thing each time: She's terribly busy and doesn't have time. 'I've done that, and it's somebody else's turn,' she said with a shrug. 'The dogs need my time and attention. They can't be left for long.'"[1]

I've heard this sentiment—"I've done that, and it's somebody else's turn"—quite often, and it strikes me as particularly sad. Allison, Graham, and Kelsey don't represent a "turn" in my life; they represent a lifelong commitment and a lifelong object of affection. That's why I feel somewhat uneasy with the phrase "raising kids." It can diminish family life to a farm activity—raising crops or raising pets. Kids are so profoundly different. I'm relating to them, caring for them, involved with them. I don't want the utilitarian aspect—growing them into adults—to become the defining point of our relationship.

Imagining life thirty years from now can help us keep the big picture in view. We can get so busy trying to make sure our children complete their homework, display good manners, not watch too much television, get enough exercise, and eat well that we can forget to enjoy them and relate to them. Kelsey's comment—"When you get to be that old, I'm going to do the ordering for you"—reminded me of the most precious aspect of parenting, namely, building a lifelong *relationship* with another human being.

This emphasis on the relationship is essential if we are to mirror the father and mother love of God. The Lord tells Israel: "Can a mother forget the baby at her breast and have no compassion on the child she has borne? Though she may forget, I will not forget you! See, I have engraved you on the palms of my hands" (Isaiah 49:15–16). Our heavenly Parent will never forget us because he has engraved us on the palms of his hands. He doesn't want us to just mind our manners and obey a few key rules; he feels passionate about getting close to us.

Likewise, our affection for our children should run deep into our very pores; it should mark our marrow and stamp our DNA. To love our kids like God loves us means they should know that our affection is as intense as it is constant. They may see our hair thinning and our minds fading, but may they never see our passion or our commitment grow dim!

Spend this week reflecting on the relationship you are building with your kids. Ask God to give you the same heart for your children that he has for you. Raising children isn't about "taking a turn"; it's about cultivating an abiding affection and a true, lifelong commitment.

*Heavenly Father, thank you for wanting to be in a close, intimate*
*relationship with us. Following your example, help us to have*
*the same kind of relationship with our children. Give us the*
*perspective to think ahead thirty years from now to the kind*
*of relationship we'll want to have. In Jesus' name, amen.*

## Questions for Reflection

1. Do you think your children feel more like projects or deeply loved children?
2. How can thinking ahead thirty or forty years from now change the way we relate to our children today?

# CRUSHED CRAYONS

*Consider it pure joy, my brothers and sisters, whenever
you face trials of many kinds, because you know
that the testing of your faith produces perseverance.
Let perseverance finish its work so that you may
be mature and complete, not lacking anything.*

JAMES 1:2–4

DR. CATHY CARPENTER IS AN ACCOMPLISHED PHYSICIAN WITH a heart for God. Her second child, Matt, was a difficult boy from day one. He became known as their "birth control baby," making both Cathy and her husband, Gordon, swear off any thoughts of having another child. Whereas Cathy and Gordon took much pride in their quiet and accommodating first child, with Matt, Cathy confesses, "I had been forced to shift to the role of trying to survive parenting."

Many people had volunteered to watch their "perfect" baby named Bethany, but *nobody* volunteered to watch Matt—even though Gordon and Cathy needed a break from him ten times more than they ever needed from Bethany. Word got around about Matt, so before long, Gordon and Cathy had to shell out serious dollars to get someone who was willing to babysit him for an evening. Matt got kicked out of his first preschool by the age of three.

Many people assumed that a difficult child meant substandard parenting. It seemed everybody had an easy solution, and they were quick to offer advice, implying that Cathy and Gordon, despite their graduate education and relative success with their compliant firstborn, didn't have a clue about what they were doing. Cathy made this wise observation:

> Parents with difficult children are special people needing support, love, and understanding. Instead, they are stranded on a desert island in a fortress of isolation with walls to the sky. They are surrounded by those well-meaning relatives, busybody friends, and complete strangers who make statements like, "Oh, he's just all boy, dear." "Why can't you control your child?" "Maybe he just eats too much sugar . . ."[1]

Matt's energy quickly became a safety issue. By the time Matt was two, he had learned how to get out of car seats. Cathy and Gordon bought three car seats with three different types of restraints, hoping to fool their two-year-old, but Matt figured his way out of each one of them in less than thirty seconds. The coup de grâce came when they finally borrowed a seat that Cathy says seemed to fit Matt like a torture chair in a James Bond movie. The chair had been specially designed to keep troublesome tykes safely in their seat. They strapped Matt in, put in a kid's music tape, and got ready for their drive out of town.

Sixty seconds later, Gordon looked in the rearview mirror and saw Matt standing straight up in the car seat, dancing and waving to the music.

Matt's energy and creativity knew no bounds. For some reason, Matt became determined to smuggle crayons into kindergarten, even though the school provided each student with his or her own crayons. After Cathy made it clear to Matt that he didn't need to take crayons to school, she noticed a bulge in his sock as she tied his shoes. Suspicious, Cathy asked Matt, "Are you hiding crayons in your socks?"

Matt defiantly stood up—how could his mother even *think* such a thing?—and watched, mortified, as crayons poured down his pants legs and out of his shirt. Cathy then did a full-body search and discovered that Matt had stashed crayons even in his underwear. She eventually counted *116 crayons* hidden in various parts of Matt's clothing!

As a young girl, older sister Bethany drew a picture of her family. Matt stood in the center of the family, his hair on end, with Gordon, Cathy, and Bethany facing Matt and looking weary. Cathy admitted, "She captured our family portrait."

What strikes me about Cathy's story is how a prominent physician and her very intelligent husband (I've met Gordon—he's on staff with a church, runs a bookstore, and is a well-read man) "always wanted to be the type of parents who remained anonymous," but whom "Matt gave the distinguished privilege of being in the speed dial format of every principal's phone system." One middle school teacher cruelly (but somewhat understandably) told Cathy, "The best part of my day is 2:30 when your son goes home."

Yet even in the midst of being misunderstood, Cathy sees much good in having such a difficult child:

> God worked in my life to change attitudes of bitterness, embarrassment, and resentment into attitudes of grace, love, and hope. These new attitudes developed out of pain, self-sacrifice, and a little creativity. God accomplished this by walking with me through the hard times I longed to control but could not. As I prayed and sought wisdom and courage, [God] placed people in my life to restore control.[2]

Just listen to Cathy's hard-won wisdom: "While people may judge us by our children's actions, God judges us by our reactions to them. I needed to stop being mortified and to start being modified. . . . At times, I actually pity those parents who have easy children. How will they ever learn these valuable lessons?"

I so appreciate Cathy's insight—that we parents need "to stop being mortified and to start being modified." It mirrors what I believe is most true about Christian family life: that God uses parenting to shape and mold us into his servants. We must learn not only how to love compliant people but also how to love difficult people, overly active people, strong-willed people, and even, on occasion, cruel people.

When we see parenting as a journey of learning how to love, the type of child we must learn to love becomes almost irrelevant. The onus of love is on the one doing the loving, not on the object of love.

*Heavenly Father, how do you want to modify me? What is it about loving others that you want this child to teach me? Where do I fall short? Where is my heart weak and immature? Point out my sin, my pride, my selfishness— and use this child to make me strong and holy in you. Thank you, Lord, for the grace of this difficult child who can teach me how to love. Amen.*

## Questions for Reflection

1. Every child is difficult in his or her own way to some degree. How has God used some of the difficulties of your children to help you grow in your ability to love imperfect or troublesome people?

2. Cathy reached a turning point when she realized she needed to stop being "mortified" and to start being "modified." How can you encourage each other to be more concerned with your response and less concerned with other people's judgments?

# 18

# HATING SIN

> *[Job's] sons used to hold feasts in their homes on their*
> *birthdays, and they would invite their three sisters to*
> *eat and drink with them. When a period of feasting*
> *had run its course, Job would make arrangements for*
> *them to be purified. Early in the morning he would*
> *sacrifice a burnt offering for each of them, thinking,*
> *"Perhaps my children have sinned and cursed God*
> *in their hearts." This was Job's regular custom.*
>
> JOB 1:4–5

JOB HATED SIN AND FEARED GOD. WHAT A POWERFUL MES-
sage Job's example must have passed on to his children, especially when
they saw how earnestly he contended for their salvation and spiritual
health. Surely, they must have known. Surely, they must have talked
among themselves: "Did you hear how Dad went home and offered a
sacrifice in case one of us got a little too loose at the party last night and
sinned against God?"

What do my kids see me getting passionate about? Do they watch
as I enthusiastically praise an athletic performance or an A+ on a math
test, while at the same time minimizing an act of disrespect toward

their mom or of cruelty toward a sibling? Or do they see me even inviting sin into my home, acting as though sinful influences won't affect their souls and weaken their spiritual resolve? Do my children think I *hate* sin? Or do they see me tolerate it, maybe even occasionally enjoy it?

Job knew well the toll that sin can exact from a human life. Even without our New Testament perspective—that Jesus Christ came to destroy sin—Job zealously tried to root it out of his life and his family. Sometimes, I think we simply forget how utterly loathsome and destructive sin can be. When we model a holy hatred of sin, we can spare our children much of the pain that sin brings.

Take lust, for example. Lust will lead our children to forsake the modesty, purity, and innocence that will bless their sexual experience once they get married. Lust may result in a lifelong disease or an out-of-wedlock pregnancy. It may blind them with misguided priorities just when they need to make wise choices as they decide on their spouses. It will certainly leave spiritual scars. It is my duty as a parent to warn my children while they are adolescents, every bit as much as it was my duty to warn them when they were toddlers that a hot stove will burn their hands.

My wife and I once attended a public performance and watched with great distraction and discomfort as a single Christian teen got virtually mauled with hand caresses by her boyfriend. This young man had no reverence, no sense of discretion, no hesitation in claiming this young woman's body as his own. The young woman's father sat right there and later even brought up the matter in a conversation: "Well, what can you do?" he said, laughing.

Contrast this with my friend Dave Dickson, a high school teacher. Dave's son is a star athlete (as a high school junior, he was offered a four-year full scholarship to play college basketball), a musician who has cut his own CD, and a guy who could pretty much take his pick of dates. But he has decided not to date, and he has never gone to a high school dance.

I asked Dave about this, and he explained, "As a teacher, I've been to those dances, and they're not a place my son needs to be."

The cavalier "boys will be boys" approach demonstrated by the first father is the polar opposite of that taken by Job and Dave. The latter two understood—and applied—a more God-honoring approach to sin.

I'm sympathetic to those parents who want to avoid an overtly negative piety that defines Christianity only by what we *don't* do. If we err in emphasis, I hope we err in preaching the positive glories and goodness of God—his mercies, his kindnesses, his comfort, his love, his gentleness, his grace. But we mustn't do this to the exclusion of warning our children (and ourselves) of the horrors of sin. Much of what we are told to avoid will seriously wound us if we fail to obey (or in our case, to warn). Charles Spurgeon reminds us, "To be a believer in God early in life is to be saved from a thousand regrets."[1]

Spiritually healthy children grow up with a keen awareness that they will always have a Loyal Friend, a True Companion, and a Trusted Savior—*and* that they have a vicious enemy, a lying opponent, and a twisted deceiver who seeks to lure them away from God's plan, purpose, and joy for their lives. His first tool is the deceitful ruse called sin, making an activity seem fun and exciting when in actuality it will bring heartache, pain, and regret.

I want my children to focus on the Loyal Friend 90 percent of the time—but I don't want them to completely forget about the twisted deceiver. I want to be like Job, who models his hatred of sin, who demonstrates to his children how sin is their enemy—an enemy not to be taken lightly. I want this to be, as it was for Job, my "regular custom."

This week, let's consider how we can model an appropriate and holy hatred of sin.

*Lord Jesus, let us remember the price you paid to bring forgiveness of sins and to break the power of sin over us. Give us your hatred of sin, and let that hatred be a warning and a refuge for our children. In your name we pray, amen.*

## Questions for Reflection

1. How can parents balance the wonder of Christian freedom and grace with a healthy hatred of sin?
2. Where do you (or each of you) tend to err when it comes to not confronting sin, or perhaps focusing on sin too much?

# 19

# ELEVEN-MINUTE SHOWERS

*So Jacob served seven years to get Rachel,*
*but they seemed like only a few days to*
*him because of his love for her.*

GENESIS 29:20

"ELEVEN MINUTES."

Jim tapped his watch and pointed in the direction of a downstairs shower. "Sarah's been in the shower for eleven minutes."

Jim was a pastor with whom I met weekly for prayer and Bible study. At the time I had just one small child, who needed to be bathed about every half hour. Hearing about a kid who cleans herself sounded to me like it was right next door to heaven. Jim's face, however, showed the taut signs of prolonged frustration. I had no idea how long showers for thirteen-year-olds were supposed to last, but Jim's tone made it clear that eleven minutes breached the limit.

As years passed and I became the bearer of a mortgage and the father of even more kids than Jim had, I began to understand Jim's concern. I found myself coming home from work and being able to spot my house a mile away—it was the one with every light on.

One day, Lisa found me going from room to room, muttering under my breath, and she asked me what was wrong.

"Nothing," I said. "I'm just trying to find a light bulb that's not turned on. I don't want it to feel left out."

Several years later, Sarah was ready to begin her first year in college. Jim and his wife had two daughters and an unusually close family, so all four of them got into the car for the two-day trip out to school. They stopped midway at a campground, and as Jim sat in front of the campfire, it suddenly hit him: *Sarah won't be living with me anymore.* Living on a tight pastor's salary, Jim couldn't afford to fly Sarah home before Christmas break. Many months ago, the fourteen weeks of separation didn't sound all that long; now, it felt like a decade.

Jim's water and electric bills would surely go down, but as he recounted the emotions of that parting, I had the feeling that having a little extra money in the bank account would feel like small consolation, indeed.

My own revelation occurred back when I worked outside the home. My kids were young enough that my evening arrival still generated a big splash. I could hear the peals of delight as soon as I got out of my car, and I almost never made it through the front door without having to step over three tiny bodies.

One winter evening, I drove up to the house, and there wasn't a single light on. At first I thought there must have been a power outage or something, but our neighbors' homes were lit up.

I walked into an empty house. Lisa and the kids had visited some friends and were stuck in traffic. The silence felt overwhelming. The house, dark and empty, looked like a completely different place. I did something I thought I'd never do. I turned most of the lights on to welcome Lisa and the kids home.

That incident became one of those "lightning" moments when God impresses a truth on your heart, when the mundane becomes prophetic and time stops long enough for a profound thought to slip through. I couldn't articulate the thought, but I realized that every blessing comes with a burden.

If God were to take my wife and children home, I'd have a much smaller electric bill—and a hole in my heart the size of Texas.

I soon realized that in just about every complaint lies the foundation of thanksgiving. The fact that you're upset because of a rainy day is due in part to the fact that you're physically able to go outside and enjoy the weather. Talk to a person who's confined to a hospital, and you won't find someone complaining about the weather.

The fact that you're so busy assumes you have a job. The fact that there's a load of laundry means someone is alive to get it dirty. The fact that you have problems at church means people are actually coming to your church.

It really comes down to how we choose to look at it. God could remove the burden—but if he did, he'd also take away the blessing. Jacob worked seven long years to marry Rachel—but because of his love for her, those seven years seemed like less than seven days. He didn't see the burden; he remained fascinated by the blessing.

This week, whenever you feel tempted to complain because your kids are being kids—making messes, not replacing the toilet paper, leaving the lights on, messing up your car—ask God to remind you of the blessing behind the burden. A clean house, a smaller bill, and a spotless car aren't nearly as satisfying as a family filled with love.

*Heavenly Father, please help us to recognize the blessing behind every burden. Help us to be thankful that we have children who make messes and responsibilities that make us tired. To remove every burden would be to remove many blessings. Thank you for the fullness of family life. In Jesus' name, amen.*

## Questions for Reflection

1. Do you have the equivalent of Jim's "eleven-minute shower"—a frustration about parenting that will likely look very different when your child leaves home? How can Jim's journey impact your perspective?

2. Consider the two or three things that most bother you about parenting; now talk about the blessings behind those burdens.

# HUMBLE PIE

*Since we have these promises, dear friends, let us purify
ourselves from everything that contaminates body and
spirit, perfecting holiness out of reverence for God.*

2 CORINTHIANS 7:1

OUR HOUSE HAS THREE LEVELS. AMAZINGLY, WHEN THE PHONE
rings, any available phone seems always at least two levels away—even
if I'm on the middle floor! That may sound impossible, physics-wise,
but, you see, I always guess wrong; I run downstairs, thinking that's
where the phones are, only to discover they're all on the top floor, which
means I have to go downstairs one flight and upstairs two flights. If
I guess upstairs, the phones will almost certainly all be downstairs,
tucked conveniently under the couch cushions or thoughtfully kicked
under the computer desk.

Oh, and all this running has to be completed within four rings.

I got so frustrated over this seemingly immutable law that I bought
five phones (three cordless and two stationary) to cover our three levels.
Did you catch that? *Five* phones, *three* levels. I figured if I bought enough
phones, eventually one of them would have to remain on each level.

But no! We regularly miss calls because all the cordless phones somehow find themselves in the same corner, buried under a pile of laundry or a kid's gym bag. Just last weekend, during a garage sale, a woman asked to borrow our phone. It took me almost ten minutes to locate a single one I could carry outside. I eventually found *two* cordless phones in one unnamed child's bedroom—one phone jammed between the wall and the back of her bed, the other buried under a huge cabinet. Of course, she had "no idea" who put them there.

One afternoon, after missing yet another call following a mad dash up the stairs, my frustration reached a breaking point. "Look," I complained to my wife and kids, "we have at least one phone for each floor. How difficult is it to leave the phone on the floor where you found it? Huh? How difficult is that? This is the *black* phone. It stays on *this* floor!"

"Gary," Lisa said, "*you* were the last one to use that phone. Remember? You had a call about a half hour ago, and you took it upstairs where it was quieter. *You're* the one who left it upstairs."

Boy, the kids had a good laugh about that one—and I could say nothing in my defense. Lisa had caught me red-handed.

As parents, it is so easy to act as though we never make mistakes, as though *we* have arrived and only our children need to get in line and then family life will be so much more pleasant. Instead of focusing on "purifying ourselves," to use Paul's language, we want to purify *him* or *her*.

It's somewhat of an occupational hazard of parenting to arrogantly forget that God is working on *all* of us. While it surely is our job to train our children, we must not forget that *we* need training too. We're not perfect role models sent to straighten out our kids; we're a family of sinners, all of whom are in need of encouragement and instruction as we seek God's grace to grow in mercy.

The Bible describes character growth as an active, lifelong pursuit.

Paul wrote to the Corinthians that we are called to a process of "*per-fecting* holiness" (2 Corinthians 7:1, emphasis added). When we act as though we've arrived, we model to our children that spiritual growth is a passing phase rather than a call that orders our entire lives. I love Andrew Murray's take on this: "As long as we are content with just enough religion to save ourselves and our children, we must not be surprised if they remain unsaved. It is only as we *seek to be filled with the Spirit* and to have our whole life sacrificed for the Kingdom, that we may count on the blessing of successful spiritual training for our children."[1]

I want my kids to see me growing day by day. I want to model to them the dynamic reality of a heart seized by God that is being molded and transformed right in front of their eyes. That reality begins with an admission that I'm a work in progress, and it continues when I recognize that, while I have authority as the parent, I'm also their brother in Christ. God is using them to teach *me* as I teach them. Remember, Jesus placed a *child* in front of the adults when he said, "This is your role model to enter the kingdom of God" (Matthew 18:3–4, personal paraphrase).

Yeah, I had a good slice of humble pie that day. But spiritually speaking, it was one of the best meals I've had in years.

This week, let's model the process of "perfecting holiness." Let's stop looking only at where our children fall short, and start looking at purifying *ourselves*. Let's allow our kids to witness firsthand how God shapes a soul, and thereby teach them what it really means to be filled, *continually* filled, with God's Holy Spirit.

> *Heavenly Father, thank you for the grace that allows us to freely admit where we fall short. Give us hearts that desire to "perfect" holiness, and eyes that are ever open to the lessons you want to teach us in the daily course of family life. In Jesus' name, amen.*

## Questions for Reflection

1. Is spiritual growth an *active* pursuit in your life, or do you tend to think that spiritual growth is automatic?

2. What do you think Andrew Murray means when he contrasts "just enough religion" to save ourselves and our children, and a life that seeks to be filled with the Spirit?

# THE HAPPIEST DAY AND
# THE BIGGER BLOW

*Do nothing out of selfish ambition or vain
conceit. Rather, in humility value others above
yourselves, not looking to your own interests
but each of you to the interests of the others.*
PHILIPPIANS 2:3–4

IN THE EIGHTEENTH CENTURY, A WOULD-BE ASSASSIN PLUNGED
a knife into the unsuspecting King Louis XV. Though the wound wasn't
mortal, doctors initially feared it was (and almost made it so, by—get
this—bleeding a man who had already lost great quantities of blood).

The king of France assumed the worst. He called for his son and
handed him the key to his writing desk.

"My son," the king said, "this now concerns you. May you be happier than I was. I'm leaving you the kingdom at a very critical moment.
I hope you'll have enough insight to govern for the best."

The king's son took his father's hands, kissed them, and mumbled
in his grief and tears, "Would to God that *I* had received the blow!"

"That would have been far more painful for me!" the king replied.

Here is a man on top of the world, living in unparalleled luxury and power and prestige. He could take (and often did) virtually any woman of his choosing; he could kill (and sometimes did) any enemy he hated. Like Israel's King Solomon, he denied himself little. And yet this man said he would much rather forfeit his own fortune than to watch his son fall before him.

I think just about any parent can relate to this. We almost take it for granted. A maturing process in parenting takes us obsessively selfish people, consumed with our own welfare, and turns us into altruistic saints. When we admit that we would willingly give up our lives so that another might live, we are saying that parenting has made us a little more like our blessed Savior, who gave his life so that his spiritual children could live: "Have the same mindset as Christ Jesus: . . . he made himself nothing, . . . by becoming obedient to death—even death on a cross!" (Philippians 2:5, 7, 8).

Bing Crosby's widow told how the famous entertainer once called her on the phone—he couldn't wait until he got home to relay the news—and said, "This is the happiest day of my life."

"Oh, what happened, darling?" she asked.

"Nathaniel [the Crosbys' son] just won the men's club championship at the Burlingame Country Club."

Bing's widow declared, "That was Bing's happiest day. Not the songs or the films or any of his show business successes. Not our wedding. . . . The fact that his teenage son had become the men's [golf] champion at the Burlingame Country Club."

Once again, a man of great accomplishment and fame found his greatest joy in a relatively small feat performed by his son. At one time, Bing had the highest-selling single ("White Christmas") of all time; country club championships are to sports achievement what Cup-a-Soup is to fine dining. Yet Bing gladly chose the lesser over the greater because the lesser had been accomplished *by his son*.

We find far more joy in feeling happy for our children than in rejoicing in our own accomplishments. Being a parent matures us by taking us from the adolescent stage of putting ourselves first and measuring everything against ourselves to finally caring more about someone else.

More and more young couples seem to be talking about never having children; they cite the costs, the hassle, and the disruption of their recreational lives. Financially, they may well come out "ahead" by remaining childless. They will probably have less heartache, certainly more peace and quiet, and undoubtedly more flexibility in their schedules. They may well be able to sign up more clients, perhaps design a better printer, or sell a few more copies of software.

But they don't have a clue about what they'll be missing spiritually.

Though at times dying to ourselves can feel very painful, it is the most liberating spiritual experience we can know. One of God's most effective ways to accomplish this process is by giving us children, who, by their very presence, invite us to finally put someone's welfare ahead of our own.

Of course, it overreaches the case a bit to assume that this journey from narcissism to altruism is a given for all parents—it's not. But that's our assignment for this week. Are we making this journey? Are we crossing this bridge? Or are we blinded by resentment for what these children take out of us and obsessed with what we must give up as we selfishly try to preserve our own welfare?

Let's allow God to use our kids to bless us and spiritually prepare us by chipping away at our narcissism. Let's lean in to this effect and embrace putting ourselves last. Since narcissism is such a potent enemy to kingdom service, our children do us a great service when they steal our hearts and finally lead us to consider someone else's welfare and achievements as more important than our own.

*Heavenly Father, we never knew we could care so much until you placed children in our home. Thank you for showing us how others' welfare can matter even more than our own. Enlarge our hearts so that we can bring that same attitude to others outside our home. In Jesus' name, amen.*

## Questions for Reflection

1. Discuss how caring about your children so much has confronted your narcissism and turned you into a more altruistic person.
2. How can we take this important lesson gleaned from parenting—caring about others' accomplishments even more than our own—and see it extend outside our kids, truly becoming even more like Jesus?

# 22

# FARSIGHTED

*Do not love the world or anything in the world.*
*If anyone loves the world, love for the Father is*
*not in them. For everything in the world—the*
*lust of the flesh, the lust of the eyes, and the pride*
*of life—comes not from the Father but from the*
*world. The world and its desires pass away, but*
*whoever does the will of God lives forever.*

1 John 2:15–17

"Parents of gifted children think ten, maybe twenty, years down the road. Parents like us think one hundred years ahead."

Alan and Lindsey have a fifteen-year-old boy named Robby. The best way to describe Robby is that he's slow. He was slow to crawl, slow to speak, slow to read, and slow to catch on to social situations. He has a hard time participating in conversations with his peers because language is so difficult for him that he'll come in at awkward moments of the conversation—say, five minutes after a topic has already passed, he'll bring it up again, out of the blue. His friends look at him like he's weird.

"They just don't understand," Alan explained, "that Robby has been working really hard for those five minutes to think of something so that he can participate in the conversation."

When Robby was younger, he had several friends, but most of them have fallen away by now. When more complicated social situations revealed Robby's slowness, the friends found new companions who could keep up. "A couple boys may still call him once or twice a year out of pity," Alan said, "but Robby's pretty much on his own."

Alan added, "With your kids, you probably think five or ten years ahead—high school graduation, marriage, a job, grandkids, stuff like that. We have to be honest—Robby's high school diploma will be marked with more concessions than a Middle East peace plan. College is not in his future. It's difficult to imagine him ever getting married, and most of the counselors we work with concede that, while Robby may find a vocation, it's unlikely it'll ever be one that pays him enough to support himself, much less a family.

"For a while, Lindsey and I kept living with the loss, but finally I understood we need to be more farsighted. Robby's gift to the world is that he teaches us this world isn't always 'fair,' and that this age isn't the end of the story. Some kids, by their gifting, point to this world; others, by what they lack, point to heaven. Robby may not have many friends down here; he may not enjoy the intimacy of marriage or the pleasure of holding a newborn son or daughter, but the pleasures of this world, as rich as they may be, don't even compare with the wonderful realities waiting for us in heaven. I was always so focused on this world with the other kids that I almost never thought about heaven. That's not the case with Robby. With him, I think about heaven all the time."

I asked Alan what helped him to turn this corner, to become "farsighted" in a world of "nearsighted" parents. He came back the next day and showed me a copy of Jonathan Edwards's *Heaven: A World of Love*.

Edwards has often been called the last of the Puritans and America's greatest intellect.

Alan took me through some passages that spoke most deeply to him. In one chapter, Edwards wrote, "There are none but lovely objects in heaven. No offensive or unlovely or polluted person or thing is to be seen there. . . . And there is nothing that is deformed with any natural or moral deformity; but everything is beautiful to behold and amiable and excellent in itself."[1]

"The day is coming," Alan explained, "when Robby's disabilities will fall away. He'll laugh right on cue instead of three minutes after everybody else has moved on from the joke. For the first time, the beauty of his glorified heavenly body will lead others to admire him instead of to look at him like he's weird while they try to figure out what's wrong with him."

"Now get this," Alan gushed. He reads from another chapter, "Love in heaven is always mutual. It is always met with appropriate returns of love. . . . No inhabitants of that blessed world will ever be grieved with the thought that they are slighted by those that they love, or that their love is not fully and fondly returned."

"Do you have any idea how many times my and Lindsey's hearts have been broken as we've watched Robby call a friend; to wince through an insecure, hard-to-understand phone call; and then for us to see that hurt look on his face as he senses his former friends pulling away? In heaven, all that will be over. He'll never be slighted; his love will always be, as Edwards puts it, 'fondly returned.'"[2]

The types of kids with glowing accomplishments—the ones about whom many parents fill their Christmas letters—*do* tend to make us shortsighted. We can become obsessed with their recreational abilities, their educational achievements, their future family life opportunities, or their vocational possibilities. But every now and then, God sends a kid who has none of that, who breaks his or her parents' hearts with the sadness they face but who can expand their souls with the truth that this world, and all that is in it, is passing away.

"Do not love the world or anything in the world," John tells us. "If anyone loves the world, love for the Father is not in them. For everything in the world—the lust of the flesh, the lust of the eyes, and the pride of life—comes not from the Father but from the world. The world and its desires pass away, but whoever does the will of God lives forever." (1 John 2:15–17).

If we're not careful, we can be so enamored by this world's promises and pleasures and cycles that we forget we don't belong here. Thanks be to God, there *is* great glory and beauty in this world! There can be great happiness, great excitement, and great meaning. But as believers, we must remember that for which God created us, the glorious hope on which all our hopes are based: "And this is what he promised us— eternal life" (1 John 2:25).

Parents whose kids "fit in" with this world may become so preoccupied with this world that they forget, or neglect, to prepare them for the next world—and what a tragedy that would be—to have kids who "succeed" at a life that will last a mere eighty or ninety years but who forfeit the world without end because they became too nearsighted.

Thank God for the kids who don't let us forget what really matters: "But many who are first will be last, and many who are last will be first" (Matthew 19:30).

Every difficulty and disappointment in our children's lives, as hard as they are for us to bear, can remind us to become more farsighted in our parenting. This world is important, but it won't be the last chapter in our kids' lives; in fact, it's barely even an introduction.[3]

*Heavenly Father, we are so grateful that, in many ways, this life is just the beginning. You have tremendous plans for the new heavens and the new earth, and we thank you for the hope that promised future brings and the comfort it gives to present disappointments. In Jesus' name, amen.*

## Questions for Reflection

1. How can the future hope of a perfect world encourage us as we watch our children face disappointment, personal limitations, and failure?
2. How should the promise of such a future impact the way we raise our children in this world?

**23**

# THE VICE OF THE VIRTUOUS

*Therefore, as God's chosen people, holy and dearly loved, clothe yourselves with compassion, kindness, humility, gentleness and patience. Bear with each other and forgive one another if any of you has a grievance against someone. Forgive as the Lord forgave you. And over all these virtues put on love, which binds them all together in perfect unity.*

COLOSSIANS 3:12–14

WE HEAR SO MUCH TALK TODAY ABOUT THE *MESSAGE* OF Christianity—a very important discussion, to be sure. We also hear a great deal about the *methods* of our faith—how to share with non-believers, how to pray, how to handle our finances, and so forth. But what often gets lost is a proper emphasis on the *manner* of our faith—how believing in God changes the way we act toward others and molds our dispositions.

Henry Drummond, author of the nineteenth-century classic *The Greatest Thing in the World*, warns us against a harsh, irritable, and impatient disposition:

The peculiarity of ill temper is that it is the vice of the virtuous. It is often the one blot on an otherwise noble character. You know men who are all but perfect, and women who would be entirely perfect, but for an easily ruffled, quick-tempered, or "touchy" disposition. This compatibility of ill temper with high moral character is one of the strangest and saddest problems of ethics.[1]

Here's where parenting can help us take that next step in spiritual formation, for parenting certainly exposes an ill-tempered or touchy disposition like nothing else. To be a parent is to be provoked. Kids regularly tend to bring out the best *and* the worst in us. If we have an ill temper, if we're touchy or edgy, raising children will certainly reveal our weakness.

Sadly, an ill manner often isn't considered a serious failing. On the contrary, we're quick to excuse ourselves in a way we'd never excuse other sins. We say, "I was overly tired and stressed, that's all." And yet, would we excuse getting drunk in front of our children simply because we were under a lot of stress? We would never think to use crude and lewd language, no matter how tired we're feeling. We wouldn't condone physical violence, even if our kids had made us *really* angry, because we believe these faults are all prohibited by the well-known message and methods of our faith.

But verbal violence? Easy irritability? These we pass over as if they were of no account, because today's believing community tends to pay far too little attention to the *manner* of our faith. Are we modeling to our children the spirit of Christ that responds to others the same way he did—with gentleness and patience? When you think about it, few things are as important as this, because our goal is to get our children to fall in love with God. What better way to do this than to model his most lovely qualities—gentleness, grace, mercy, and patience?

Drummond gave this timely reminder:

> No form of vice, not worldliness, not greed of gold, not drunkenness itself, does more to un-Christianize society than evil temper. For embittering life, for breaking up communities, for destroying the most sacred relationships, for devastating homes, for withering up men and women, for taking the bloom off childhood; in short, for sheer gratuitous misery-producing power, this influence stands alone.[2]

Are we "taking the bloom off" our children's childhood by stalking around in surly moods? Are we unleashing "misery-producing power" by failing to keep our tempers in check? Are we withering other family members with our icy blasts of ill will? Have we addressed our *manner* of living?

How do we deal with our ill temper? The best antidote is *humility*. When we possess an attitude of repentance, remembering how much God has forgiven us, always being sensitive to how mercifully he has treated us and being thankful for the grace he showers on us, we feel compelled from within to likewise be forgiving, merciful, and gracious to others. When repentance dies in our lives, legalistic and perfectionistic faultfinding is born. Instead of remaining sensitive to God's grace, we become sensitive about every little slight, every little irritation, anything that might bring the smallest amount of discomfort or distraction. When we don't live as a people in need of grace, we expect others to be perfect, and we bitterly resent it whenever even the slightest imperfection puts us out.

Drummond counsels that "souls are made sweet not by taking the acid fluids out, but by putting something in—a great Love, a new Spirit, the Spirit of Christ. Christ, the Spirit of Christ, interpenetrating ours, sweetens, purifies, transforms all." In other words, we become yielded worshipers, regularly putting ourselves before the presence of God, allowing his Spirit to penetrate our hearts and transform our manner from the inside out. Parenting is a busy task, and this world is a busy world, but we must be careful that worship does not become a casualty in our schedules, because if we are not regularly and consistently filled with God, our homes will become regularly and consistently filled with hatred, accusation, judgment, venom, and impatience—all the ugly, soul-crippling qualities of ill temper.

Begin this week in your heavenly Father's presence, asking him to fill you with the sweet attitudes of Christ. You've taught your kids the gospel message—good for you! You've told them how to pray and urged them to tithe out of their allowance—excellent! Now model the manner of their faith. Demonstrate the loveliness of God's disposition toward us, so they'll fall in love, not just with what God has said and done, but with who he *is*.

*Heavenly Father, help us to receive your grace and help us to experience your gentle manner, so that we may pass on the loveliness of who you are to our children. We want to love them and each other in the same manner as you love us. In Jesus' name, amen.*

## Questions for Reflection

1. Do you see God as a gentle God? Read Matthew 11:29 and talk to each other about Jesus' gentle nature.
2. How can we reconcile the gentleness of Christ with his sometimes bold confrontations? What does that balance teach us about raising our children?
3. In what areas is it most difficult for you to be gentle with your children? How can you encourage each other during these times?

# CURSED SILENCE

*And the things you have heard me say in the*
*presence of many witnesses entrust to reliable*
*people who will also be qualified to teach others.*
2 TIMOTHY 2:2

IN HIS POIGNANT MEMOIR *MY LOSING SEASON*, PAT CONROY recalls how important basketball was to him as a boy. Since Pat's father served in the military, Pat moved from town to town. The one constant in his life, the one place he felt at home, was on the basketball court. It didn't matter what state he lived in—the basket always remained ten feet off the ground. The free throw line was always fifteen feet away. And four teammates always surrounded him.

Conroy's father was a star player in his own right. Indeed, in Pat's words, "He is still considered, by some, to be the best basketball player to attend St. Ambrose College . . . and his name hangs in its Athletic Hall of Fame."[1]

Then, in one of the saddest paragraphs of literature I've read in some time, Conroy describes how *little* his father did with this skill:

> With my father's great gifts, he could've taught me everything about
> basketball I'd need to know. . . . Instead, he taught me nothing, and I

went to the Citadel not knowing what a pivot was or how to block out on a rebound or how to set a pick to free a teammate for a shot or how to play defense. A beautiful shooter, a fierce rebounder, and a legendary defender, my father chose not to pass these ineffable skills on to any of his five sons. We grew up overshadowed by his legend, and that legend did not lift a finger to help us toward any patch of light our own small achievements might have granted us.[2]

What inheritance has God given to us that we are hoarding and not passing on to our children? God told Abraham he had been blessed to be a blessing (Genesis 12:2); Paul told Timothy he was to "entrust" others with the teaching he had received (2 Timothy 2:2). Both Old and New Testaments urge us to serve as faithful conduits and messengers, passing on whatever favor God has shown to us.

Maybe, like me, you have little basketball knowledge to pass on to your kids. But what have you learned about prayer? About relationships? About marriage? About handling finances? About friendships?

God has patiently tutored us in all these areas. Sometimes, we've learned the hard way, through broken relationships or mountains of debt. But whatever we've learned, we have a spiritual obligation to pass on to our children. I don't always feel like I have all that much to give— but it's my responsibility to give them everything I *do* have.

I remember the time Graham came home after being asked to give a short talk to his youth group. "Can you help me, Dad?" he asked.

I'll never be able to help Graham fix a car, do any serious plumbing, or build a house, but I *could* help him give a talk. We discussed the importance of the opening, why he needed to make just a few clear points, and, most important, how he needed to ask in any talk, "Where is the point where God is glorified?"

Sadly, we've passed through a largely silent generation of parents.

Many kids have been allowed to go their own way. They haven't been challenged, and they haven't been taught. In my "Sacred Marriage" seminars, I ask the wives to raise their hands if they were trained by older women to love their husbands and children, as Paul prescribes in Titus 2:4; in a group of several hundred women, maybe two or three will raise their hand.

I'm just as guilty. I've talked to thousands about how God has challenged me with regard to cultivating a gentle spirit. I've written a chapter on that very topic in one of my books. And yet I watched as one of my children was growing up with the tendency to take offense very easily, and I realized I was neglecting to pass on to this child what I had entrusted to others. I was hoarding a skill that can produce rich benefits for every marriage or parenting relationship. Thankfully, this child was young enough for me to get a second chance.

May this cursed silence stop! Sacred parenting teaches us to be active, to initiate, to leave behind a rich spiritual inheritance. No more hoarding! Freely we have received; freely let us give.

It will take years to pass on all we've been given, but certainly this idea of an intentional transfer should remain a persistent purpose of parenting. We should look for opportunities to give our kids whatever we have. Don't fret over what you *can't* give them; if you're truly faithful to pass on what you do have, you'll run out of time before you run out of wisdom.

*Heavenly Father, help us to be more intentional about purposefully transferring all that you've given us to the next generation. Help us to see the unique understanding and skills you've entrusted to us, and make us faithful to share them with our children. In Jesus' name, amen.*

## Questions for Reflection

1. This week, take an inventory: What has God given you—things unique to your experience and training—that you can pass on to your children? Are you an athlete, a handyman, a culinary artist, a gardening genius, a natural artist? What have you learned about men and women, about life goals, about friendships and faith? About prayer, about God, about worship, and about sharing your faith?

2. Talk about how the two of you can be more intentional about the active, training aspect of parenting. Which child can benefit most from which gift that God has given you?

# 25

# STOP JUDGING AND START LOVING

*Jesus answered, . . . "You judge by human standards; I pass judgment on no one."*
JOHN 8:14–15

CATHY ONCE ACCOMPANIED HER DAUGHTER, JAMIE, ON A school trip to Europe. Jamie suffers from obsessive-compulsive disorder (OCD), and she was taking prescription medication that sometimes causes a psychotic reaction—which had the unhappy effect of making Jamie even more of an outcast among the kids than she already was.

Cathy watched as the other kids on the trip either ignored Jamie or made fun of her. It's not as though Cathy couldn't see that Jamie was different: her gait, her attitude, and the volume of her voice gave cruel kids more than enough fodder for their ridicule. Objectively, Cathy could see why her daughter was ostracized and ridiculed; subjectively, it still hurt.

If you've never felt truly embarrassed by one of your kids, you probably can't imagine what Cathy endured. She loved Jamie, but she felt frustrated by her daughter's behavior and the bizarre way the drugs and the OCD interacted in her system. She tried to maintain a positive attitude, but the symptoms of children who face psychotic challenges can wear you down. It's one thing to relate to a mentally challenged kid for an hour, a day, or even a week—but when it goes on and on and on with virtually no break, you can reach a point where you feel pushed beyond your limit. After months and then years of dealing with it, you can snap.

One day, Cathy reached that limit. To her own horror, she heard herself scold Jamie, "Why can't you just be normal?"

The words hung in the air long after she had spoken them. Shocked, saddened, and hurt by her own behavior, Cathy realized she had just done the same thing as the kids—faulting Jamie for not being "normal."

We've all been there; whether or not we've actually verbalized our frustrations to our children, I'm sure most of us have at least *thought* them. We don't expect our kids to be perfect, but we often wish they were a little *less* imperfect than they are now, or perhaps imperfect in a different way.

Jamie has come a long way since that ninth-grade trip to Europe—but Cathy has come even further. She made this honest admission:

> What I learned from this very dark time in my life is that it was my shame and my pettiness that had to be revealed in order for me to begin to love Jamie. I was no better than those mean girls on the England trip. Sometimes I didn't try to see her side and her pain; I was too busy worrying about what others might think. I belittled her, if only in my mind. I needed to stop judging and to start loving. . . . I had to face the ugly side of my behavior, confess it, and pray for change. I had to realize that I am the broken one in need of fixing, not Jamie.

*I needed to stop judging and to start loving. . . . I had to realize that I am the broken one in need of fixing, not Jamie.* In this, Cathy has given us a golden nugget of truth. She understands a side of parenting that gets far too little attention. We get to choose our spouses, but we don't get to choose our kids (apart from adoption); they come ready-made by God with all kinds of problems attached. Our job isn't to judge them for *what they're not* but to love them *as they are.*

Your children may not have OCD, but they certainly have temper tantrums, perpetually messy rooms, selective hearing, and occasional rebellious streaks. These failings can embarrass and frustrate us. They can also tempt us to focus more on what *we're* going through than on what our kids are facing—and that's when we tend to start judging and stop loving.

What it comes down to for me is this: sometimes I simply grow weary of parenting sinners. But *every child is a sinner!* Thus every child stretches us, pushes us, challenges us, and—by God's design—teaches us how to love.

This week, every time you're tempted to think about how embarrassed you feel, how frustrated you feel, how this child tests you to no end, take a deep breath and pray, "God, how do you want me to love this child in this situation? What are her greatest needs? What don't I understand about him that makes me judge him instead of love him?"

May God grant us all the grace to become a little more like Cathy, who is determined to love, and a little less like the Pharisees, who were so eager to judge.

> *Heavenly Father, help us to receive our children, with all*
> *their innate weaknesses, with the same grace with which you*
> *receive us. Remind us that we are the ones who need "fixing,"*
> *at least as much as our children. In Jesus' name, amen.*

## Questions for Reflection

1. Do you ever find yourself wishing that your child was less imperfect, or imperfect in a different way? How can you transfer that fruitless line of thought to one of compassion for your child having to bear the burden of being made that way?

2. Do you, like Cathy, ever find yourself spending more time worrying about what others might think about your child instead of having empathy for your child? Talk about ways you can change this negative line of thinking.

3. Discuss the importance of your child feeling known, understood, accepted, and empathized with.

# QUIET

*Bring [your children] up in the training
and instruction of the Lord.*
Ephesians 6:4

Nobody warned me how noisy parenting can be. Nor was I warned about the constant interruptions. Every parent who has a kid banging on a bathroom door ten seconds after it closes knows there is no such thing as peace and solitude when toddlers fill the house.

Which is why sometimes our highest goal may simply be a day without any annoyances. But that's like joining a battle and then resenting it when bullets fly. You can't raise, much less train, sinners without regular annoyances. Yet behind every battle is a teaching opportunity, a chance to disciple living human beings.

You can't cook dinner without making at least a little mess. You can't take a shower without getting something wet. And you can't raise kids if your highest value is quiet and being left alone.

Our desire to "engage in the battle" or fantasize about peace and quiet will determine whether we'll respond to that sassing or let it slide because we don't want the hassle right now. Our answer will also determine whether we find out why our child is unusually moody or depressed—or whether we're simply thankful he or she isn't bothering us.

While quiet is certainly pleasant, we have a higher calling as Christian parents. The apostle Paul rarely addressed fathers directly, but look at the two places where he did—and see if you can find anything in common:

- Ephesians 6:4: "Fathers, do not exasperate your children; instead, bring them up in the training and instruction of the Lord."
- Colossians 3:21: "Fathers, do not embitter your children, or they will become discouraged."

Why does Paul juxtapose exasperating our children with patiently bringing them up in the training and instruction of the Lord? Why does he warn fathers, in particular, not to embitter or discourage our children?

Perhaps fathers have a natural tendency to ignore regular training or instruction until the kid's disobedience reaches a crisis point; then we respond with a verbal nuclear bomb fueled by pent-up frustration. Instead of slowly and persistently training in the daily realities of life, we keep turning a blind eye and then explode when we just can't take it anymore. In the absence of patient training, verbal explosions will become all too common. The yelling won't impress our kids, however; you can rest assured they won't listen and say, "Wow, this must really be important." Instead, they'll think, "Sheesh, doesn't *he* have a temper this morning!" After all, we've let the same behavior pass by us for weeks on end. It's only natural they'll assume the issue is our temper, not their behavior.

As long as quietness and not being bothered are our true aims, we'll be tempted to ignore the early warning signs of character going awry. Perhaps we're hoping the character flaw will go away by itself; maybe we think it's not serious enough to bother with. When the problem progresses to a crisis point, our response gets fueled primarily by irritation rather than concern. It's not motivated by justice but by anger at being put out and bothered.

Of course, this will only confuse and discourage our kids. It won't create a redemptive environment of change and transformation but one of angry outbursts, defensive posturing, and seething resentments.

Paul's call to us is much nobler. Instead of ignoring what's going wrong, we are to busy ourselves with an *ongoing* training and instruction of the Lord. We know kids don't naturally grow up holy. We know kids inherit the same sin nature we do. We know kids aren't born with an understanding of true doctrine, and that they have to learn how to cooperate with God's Holy Spirit. This type of instruction takes time and determined effort—and rarely is it "convenient." Kids tend to act up when we feel most tired, most busy, and preoccupied with something else.

Motivation is everything here. What is it that we seek in our homes? Maturity, or mere tranquility? Trained, discipled Christian workers, or sinners who have learned how far they can go without pushing their parents to react? Parenting is a process of regular disturbances for a high and noble end.

This week, ask yourself if you've fallen into the rut of thinking, "If all is quiet, all is well." We are to train and instruct our children. Training is sometimes painful, occasionally noisy, usually bothersome, and always purposeful. Let's redouble our efforts and resolve not to let potentially serious problems slide until we get so frustrated that we respond with the wrong motives and manner.

*Heavenly Father, forgive us when we value peace and quiet
over opportunities to engage and train our children. Help
us to focus on purposeful, consistent parenting, instead of
overlooking things we shouldn't, and then exploding with rage
when we've finally had enough. In Jesus' name, amen.*

## Questions for Reflection

1. Are you or your spouse particularly prone to becoming irritated when noise levels rise or in the face of constant disruptions? Do you think this is healthy? Do you need to adjust expectations or rethink your priorities?

2. Are you patiently dealing with issues as they arise instead of waiting until things get really bad? Discuss how positive training can help avoid parental "eruptions"—along the lines of "the best defense is a good offense."

# A HOUSE OF LOVE

*Dear friends, let us love one another, for love comes from God. Everyone who loves has been born of God and knows God. Whoever does not love does not know God, because God is love. . . . Dear friends, since God so loved us, we also ought to love one another. No one has ever seen God; but if we love one another, God lives in us and his love is made complete in us.*

1 JOHN 4:7–8, 11–12

WHAT MARKS A TRULY CHRISTIAN HOME? IS IT THE FACT THAT our minivan or SUV pulls out of the driveway every Sunday morning at 9:00 a.m. and heads to church?

Is it the fact that we have a Bible inside the home and some religious art on our walls?

Is it the fact that we pray before meals and at bedtime?

Let me attempt to answer this question indirectly. I enjoy reading through the great Christian classics, particularly when I notice classical writers saying almost the same thing. You get a feel for how God's Holy Spirit reveals his truth in two different eras, through different individuals, and the "testimony of two or three" becomes even more convincing than the creative words of one.

Andrew Murray would say that the true mark of a Christian home is love: "The home is consecrated by the light of Jesus' love resting on the children, the power of His love dwelling in the parents, and the raising of children being made a work of love for Him."[1] He urges parents, "Try to maintain the rule of love—not merely natural parental love, but love as a principle of action that is carefully cultivated in your family life. Then the children will catch this spirit of love and become your helpers in making your home the reflection of love for which the heavenly Father guides and trains His children."[2]

Now compare the above with Charles Spurgeon:

> The best preparation for teaching Christ's lambs is love—love for Jesus and for them. . . . Where there is no love, there will be no life. . . . We preach and teach love. Our subject is the love of God in Christ Jesus. How can we teach this if we have no love ourselves? Our object is to create love in the hearts of those we teach, and to foster it where it already exists. But how can we convey the fire if it is not kindled in our own hearts? How can a person promote the flame whose hands are damp and dripping with worldliness and indifference, so that he acts on the child's heart rather as a bucket of water than as a flame of fire?
>
> These lambs of the flock live in the love of Christ. . . . They were chosen in love and redeemed in love. They have been called in love, washed in love, and fed by love. They will be kept by love until they come to the green pastures on the hilltops of heaven. You and I will be out of gear with the vast machinery of divine love unless our souls are full of affectionate zeal for the good of the beloved ones.[3]

Both Murray and Spurgeon recognize love as the hallmark of the Christian home. We receive, celebrate, and live in God's love; we pass on that love to our children, and we teach them to love God and others. We are born in love, redeemed by love, carried by love, and called to love.

May our kids see that our primary motivation, the rule of our lives, the guiding principle in our home, is love—for in that love, they'll see the way of the kingdom and seek to know this love for themselves.

This week, consider what the level of love is in your house. More important than the color of the walls, the age of the couch, the size of the floor plan, or the acreage of the yard is the amount of love in the hearts of the parents. Remember—it's not just natural parental love, but "love as a principle of action that is carefully cultivated in your family life." Would your children see love as the ruling principle, the guiding element, the prevailing climate inside your house?

*Heavenly Father, give us a new thirst to have a home that seeks to be defined by love. Help us to receive your love and learn how to pass that love on so that, when our kids are gone, the thing they will remember most is that they grew up in a house filled with love. In Jesus' name, amen.*

## Questions for Reflection

1. What would a house "defined by love" look like in today's world? How would the parents treat and speak to the children? How would the children speak to their parents and each other?

2. Why is it so easy to focus on the physical needs of our house and children, while neglecting the most important spiritual need of love? How can you encourage each other (or remind yourself) of the need to pursue love above all else?

# THE EIGHT-POUND
# SEMINARY PROFESSOR

*Do not rebuke an older man harshly, but exhort*
*him as if he were your father. Treat younger*
*men as brothers, older women as mothers, and*
*younger women as sisters, with absolute purity.*

1 TIMOTHY 5:1–2

No, MY BABY DAUGHTER DIDN'T TEACH ME ABOUT PREDESTI-
nation or transubstantiation, or about how to parse Greek words.
But she became a seminary for my character—one that continues to
this day.

Paul talked about how God uses family life to prepare us for ministry. In fact, when talking to the young man Timothy, Paul appealed
to familial relationships: "Do not rebuke an older man harshly, but
exhort him as if he were your father. Treat younger men as brothers,
older women as mothers, and younger women as sisters, with absolute
purity" (1 Timothy 5:1–2).

Paul encouraged Timothy to draw on family life as the model for
his ministry. Certainly, Paul followed this line of thinking in his own

life. Though we have no evidence that Paul actually had children, he liked to use parenting metaphors when speaking about his own ministry. It expressed the attitude he had toward those under his care:

- "I am writing this not to shame you but to warn you as my dear children" (1 Corinthians 4:14).
- "As a fair exchange—I speak as to my children—open wide your hearts also" (2 Corinthians 6:13).
- "My dear children, for whom I am again in the pains of childbirth until Christ is formed in you" (Galatians 4:19).
- "We were like young children among you. Just as a nursing mother cares for her children" (1 Thessalonians 2:7).

The apostle John had the same attitude, confirming that this expresses the mature demeanor of one called to shepherd others:

- "And now, dear children, continue in [Jesus]" (1 John 2:28).
- "I have no greater joy than to hear that my children are walking in the truth" (3 John 4).

Even celebrities understand the positive impact of how working with children prepares us to work with adults. Singer Susanna Hoffs played with the Bangles, an all-female rock band that enjoyed considerable success in the 1980s but then broke up when the women started their families. They reunited almost ten years later, and Hoffs talked to a reporter about how different it felt being in a band *after* she had kids than before. Becoming a parent had equipped her to handle her bandmates more effectively: "If someone comes into the rehearsal studio in a cranky mood, I'm like, 'OK, are you hungry or tired? Do you need a nap? How about a cappuccino?'"[1]

Actress and writer Carrie Fisher has said, "What I know about love I learned from being a mother."[2] And Hollywood actor Jude Law confessed, "If you think it's being a man lying in bed until twelve, you ought to try getting up at seven to take care of kids. If there's anything that's going to make a man out of you, it's having your will broken by a one-year-old girl."[3]

The next time you hold a baby, think of him or her as an eight-pound seminary professor. This child will teach you about patience, service, selflessness, communication, listening skills—everything you need, character-wise, to serve God's church. When we enter parenting with the assumption that we have lessons to be learned as well as lessons to impart, God can use the process to make us into more effective ministers for his kingdom.

Cooperate with God in this aim: What does he want to teach you today? What kind of character is he going to form out of your interaction with this drooling bundle, curious toddler, or brooding teen? What type of people might he be preparing you to reach out to?

*Heavenly Father, our home is one of the best places to learn how to understand, serve, forgive, and ask forgiveness. Help us to give ourselves fully to the process of parenting so that we can increasingly become the kind of people you call us to be. In Jesus' name, amen.*

## Questions for Reflection

1. Think of the lessons you've had to learn in order to parent—confronting a child, comforting a child, praying for a child, understanding a child—how can those skills serve you as you seek to minister to others outside your home?

2. How can learning to view those we minister to as family members transform the nature of our fellowship with each other?

# 29

# BE TENDER, BUT BE TRUE

*Sin is crouching at your door; it desires to*
*have you, but you must rule over it.*
GENESIS 4:7

I LOVE TO ENCOURAGE MY CHILDREN. I CONSISTENTLY LOOK
for positive qualities and personal choices I can commend and praise.
My kids may grow weary of hearing me say, "I love you," and, "I'm proud
of you," but I'd rather they get tired of it than to never hear those phrases
at all.

But it's not the full story.

To be a *Christian* parent, I also have to tell them they're *not* okay. In
fact, they're sinners; apart from Christ, they are as dead in their transgres-
sions and sins (Ephesians 2:1) as any adult. Charles Spurgeon, who wasn't
one to mince words, blew away our sentimental notions in this regard:
"Unless you have a very clear sense of the utter ruin and spiritual death of
children, you will be incapable of being made a blessing to them."[1]

Spurgeon had much more to say about this:

> [The doctrine of the cross] will necessitate your teaching the child his
> need of a Savior. You must not hold back from this necessary task. Do
> not flatter the child with delusive rubbish about his nature being good

and needing to be developed. Tell him he must be born again. Don't bolster him up with the notion of his own innocence, but show him his sin. Mention the childish sins to which he is prone, and pray the Holy Spirit to work conviction in his heart and conscience. Deal with the young in much the same way as you would with the old. Be thorough and honest with them. Flimsy religion is good for neither young nor old. These boys and girls need pardon through the precious blood as surely as any of us.[2]

There's a reason my children fuss and fight and sass—they were born with wicked, wayward hearts. There's a reason they are selfish, impatient, and sometimes vindictive—they inherited a sin nature from their parents, and they need a Savior to change them.

If I focus only on their self-esteem in a positive sense, they may never realize their need for a Savior. "Do not hesitate to tell the child of his ruin," Spurgeon warned, "or else he will not desire the remedy. Tell him also of the punishment of sin, and warn him of its terror. Be tender, but be true. Do not hide from the youthful sinner the truth, however terrible it may be."[3]

I particularly like that phrase, "Be tender, but be true." Some of us focus only on being true, so we're never tender. Our kids tune us out because truth without love is very difficult to swallow. Others of us are so concerned about being tender that we're never true. We thus wound our kids by not giving them all the information they need. Spurgeon encourages us to be both tender and true.

In pointing to the necessity of speaking plainly about the consequences of sin, Spurgeon praised a father who all but declared his oldest son damned following an unexpected death:

The father did not, as some would have done, say to his family, "We hope your brother has gone to heaven." Instead, overcoming his natural feelings, he was enabled by divine grace to assemble his other children together and to say to them, "My sons and daughters, your brother is dead. I fear he is in hell. You knew his life and conduct. You saw how he behaved. Now God has snatched him away in his sins." Then he solemnly told them of the place of woe to which he believed—yes, with most certainty knew—his son had gone, begging them to shun it and to flee from the wrath to come.[4]

While this may sound harsh, remember that tenderness must be joined with truth: "Had he acted," wrote Spurgeon, "as some would have done, with tenderness of heart, but not with honesty of purpose, he would have said he hoped his son had gone to heaven. What would the other children have thought about that? 'If he is gone to heaven, there is no need for us to fear. We may live as we like.'"[5]

I want my children to see their promise in Jesus Christ—but I also want them to be very aware of their ruin without him. There is no hope apart from him. There is no chance they can win for themselves the ultimate victory over the base desires and rebellion they were born with.

I am called to say to my children what God said to Cain: "Sin is crouching at your door; it desires to have you, but you must rule over it" (Genesis 4:7). From Cain's subsequent murder of Abel (even after receiving this warning) and the teaching of the New Testament, we know that none of us can master sin on our own strength; but the Holy Spirit provides redemption and empowerment for those who will confess their sin, admit their hopeless state, and throw themselves on the grace of God.

In this culture, we read much about the importance of building self-esteem. There's a place for that, but not at the expense of explaining our children's desperate need for a Savior. We must be tender, but we must also be true.

*Heavenly Father, teach us to tell our children the whole truth, to find the right balance between being "tender" but also "true." We want our children to know they are loved and special, but also that they need the spiritual remedy of your Son's forgiveness. In his name we pray, amen.*

## Questions for Reflection

1. Have you spoken truth without tenderness and turned your children away? Or have you been so tender, so encouraging, that you've withheld the truth and thus put their souls in peril?

2. Do you believe your children know their need for a Savior? How can you help your children understand how to accept the fact of their sinfulness as well as the remedy offered to them in Jesus Christ?

# NOTHING IN COMMON

*Children's children are a crown to the aged.*
PROVERBS 17:6

"It's just that we have nothing in common anymore."
The man who was speaking to me was bored in his marriage and seeking a way out.

"Nothing in common?" I replied. "I thought you had two children?"

"Well, besides that."

It took all my self-restraint not to scream.

"*Besides* that?" What could be more significant, more important, more worth sacrificing for, than raising two children? What *else* do you need?

I'm serious. What will I do that is more significant than raising image bearers of the Creator God himself, future workers in his kingdom, eventual immortal rulers? What could two people ever have in common with someone other than their spouse that could possibly compete with such a bond? That one of them prefers to go camping while the other would rather stay in hotels? That one of them wants to watch romantic comedies and the other prefers science-fiction novels? That one of them wants to take lots of walks in the park and one of them is more of a homebody?

These things, even in the aggregate, pale in comparison to the joint effort of raising children. Our real crown is that we are raising children who themselves will have children. At the end of our lives, this will matter far more than what we ate for dinner or how we spent our Friday nights.

It is a serious misalignment of priorities when a couple breaks apart a family and then says, "We just don't have anything in common anymore."

In fact, *actively* raising children can do wonders for a marriage. It provides a joint task, a true friendship, a mutual challenge, which binds hearts together. Why do golfers like to hang out with other golfers? Because they can talk about certain holes ("On the eighteenth, you have to stay to the right of the fairway, or you'll never get on the green in two") and share their mutual love for the game. Book groups gather around their love for a particular genre of novel or for certain favorite authors.

These are mere hobbies that don't carry half the weight of two people energetically raising human beings. The key is that couples who say "We don't have anything in common anymore" are betraying the fact that they are not actively raising their kids together. They may be living with them, but they are not purposefully training and instructing them; otherwise, they would never even think to utter such a silly phrase.

Just this morning, our kids had an argument. Lisa addressed it first, but moments later, the argument was still raging. She came down to my office, told me what was going on, and suggested I give it a shot. I sat the involved kids down, and we read through James 4—about how quarrels and fighting reveal the sin in our hearts—and I asked each child what sin *of his or her own* was contributing to the conflict. Both children identified their sin, and then they went back to their rooms to pray through James 4 and see if they couldn't resolve the situation.

In the ideal Christian world, that would have settled it; but ten minutes after my "inspiring" meditation, they were at it *again* (so much for my preaching credentials!). Lisa took the next lesson, and we tag-teamed our way through the morning.

Certainly, a marriage is about more than raising children—but raising children is such a significant task that, when done with serious prayer, involved energy, engaged efforts, and thousands of hours of conversation, it inevitably knits two hearts together. The loyalty and friendship that such an effort engenders will run far deeper and last much longer than any temporary infatuation. By raising kids together, Lisa and I are laying the groundwork for a lifetime of genuine friendship. We have more memories than we can ever recount. We have the respect of seeing how the other stepped in when one of us was weak or faltering. We have the ongoing relationship with three younger human beings who were created in an act of love by a God of love and who were raised by parents whose love for each other grows each day. What other kind of love could ever dream of competing with that?

When you have children and leave your spouse for someone else with whom you "have more in common," know this: you are literally placing your appreciation for fine dining, recreation, old movies, or any number of comparatively insignificant preferences over the God-ordained task of loving and raising the children he has given you.

If your marriage is based merely on attraction, it will be in peril as soon as someone more attractive appears. If your marriage is only about having fun together, it will begin to wilt when you meet someone even more enjoyable and more fun to be with. But if your marriage is about raising children to the glory of God, you've just about divorce-proofed your relationship. While marriage is certainly about more than raising children, that task alone is almost enough, by itself, to keep us together. It's a glorious calling we'll never be totally worthy to fulfill.

But by God's goodness it has been given to us, and with his aid we are committed to seeing it through.

Nothing in common? Who could ever think such a thing?

*Heavenly Father, capture our minds and hearts with the immensity of all that it means to raise children together. Let us remember its importance, and help us both to give ourselves fully to that task, and then, please, draw our hearts ever closer as we face parenting together. In Jesus' name, amen.*

## Questions for Reflection

1. Are you both equally involved in parenting, or do you feel that one of you has taken on most of the responsibility?
2. How do you think that recommitting to joint parenting can bind your hearts closer to each other and rejuvenate your marriage?
3. Discuss the strengths that each of you brings to parenting, strengths that the other spouse may lack. Thank God for the way he has prepared you by joining your strengths as you seek to raise children who honor him.

# 31

# "THANKS FOR STOPPING BY"

*Better a little with the fear of the Lord*
*than great wealth with turmoil.*

PROVERBS 15:16

FORMER PGA GOLF PROFESSIONAL BRANDEL CHAMBLEE FACED a crossroads shortly after his forty-first birthday. Like most golf professionals, he was on the road half of the year—literally.

His kids took the absence personally.

"Daddy, do you like golf?" his son, Brandel Jr. (they call him "Little B"), asked him one day.

"Sure, I love golf," Brandel replied.

"Why?" Little B asked. "It takes you away from your kids."[1]

Little B didn't realize that his father's career earnings of over $4 million came with more than a few perks, including a playground the size of a Wal-Mart. "My pal, Andrew Magee, says there are only two man-made objects you can see from space—the Great Wall of China and my playground," Brandel said.

But that playground, even with its motorized car track, tunnels, slides, pool, and putting green, can't compete with Dad's presence.

One day, Brandel helped Little B build a boat for Boy Scouts. Little B talked in excited tones about racing it the next day, when Brandel broke the bad news. "Sorry, B, I'm not going to be here tomorrow when you get home from school. I've got to go to a golf tournament."

"Well," Little B replied, "thanks for stopping by."[2]

I've talked with enough kids to know that when we neglect them to provide bigger houses or better vacations, when we put them in day care at an early age so that both of us can work, the kids *never* look at it as us sacrificing for them; they see themselves as sacrifices for *us*. That's because nothing speaks so loudly to our kids as does our presence or our absence.

Brandel eventually opted to leave the PGA tour and pursue a career as a TV announcer, which keeps him away just sixty days a year instead of 180. At one time he tried to do both. Coming in from a round, a few guys asked Brandel how he had done.

"All right," he said. "I shot a 72."

Tiger Woods was sitting at a nearby table; he turned around and said, "Pretty good for a TV announcer." Then he asked, "What are you, anyway—a golfer or a TV guy?"

Brandel wrote, "Well, it's official now, Tiger. I'm a TV guy. I view it as only a part-time thing, though. My real job is to be a husband and father of three. Pardon me for smiling, but in my opinion I have the best . . . job in the world."[3]

Sounds like Brandel isn't "just stopping by" anymore; he's finally come home.

But I wonder—how about us? No, we may not travel 180 days a year, but are we checking out emotionally? Would our kids describe us as "just stopping by"? Would they ask us, "Do you like golf?" "Do you like watching *The Bachelor*?" "Do you like being so involved at church?" And then when we say yes, would they respond, "Why? It takes you away from your kids"?

This isn't to say we can't have outside interests and diversions when our children are young; you can even make the argument that an occasional break can help us be even more involved in our children's lives.

But when it starts to feel to our kids like we're just stopping by, that's the time to make some major adjustments, rethink our schedules, and give ourselves with new vigor and intention to the sacred calling of being parents first, hobbyists (and perhaps even employees) second.

*Heavenly Father, we know that parenting is a season that one day comes to an end. Help us to be faithful during this season and to make the necessary sacrifices to be there for our children as much as possible. In Jesus' name, amen.*

## Questions for Reflection

1. Where are you most invested, emotionally speaking? Is it a hobby? A job? Or is it your family?
2. How can you better balance the need to provide for your children financially while also being there for them emotionally?

# 32

# CROSS APPOINTMENTS

*"Whoever wants to be my disciple must deny themselves
and take up their cross daily and follow me."*
LUKE 9:23 (EMPHASIS ADDED)

IN 1924, THE THEN-TWENTY-SIX-YEAR-OLD C. S. LEWIS TOOK
in the mother of a friend who had died in the war. His relationship with
Mrs. Moore was frequently a difficult one. Finances were tight, and
they had no domestic help. As Lewis performed his academic duties,
Mrs. Moore had a strict opinion of how he should help around the
house.

One day, young Lewis had just about reached his limit. After doing
some shopping, he no sooner arrived home than he got sent back out
to deliver a message. After these two trips, Mrs. Moore met him with
a cross word for not taking the dog along with him in order to give
the animal some exercise. In his diary, Lewis wrote, "After lunch the
nervous irritation bottled up inside me reached such a pitch and my
thoughts became so irresponsible and foolish and so out of control that
for a moment I was really afraid that I was going into hysteria."[1]

Lewis felt so frustrated and enraged that he could scarcely manage
it. But in the turmoil he had to pass through, a mature Christian leader

was being shaped—a man unusually in touch with the vagaries of the human heart and the complexities of the human soul. Lewis had to learn how to die so that he could learn how to live. Lewis's biographer George Sayer observed, "Later on, [Lewis] came to regard domestic life as a school of virtue. He found it quite hard to acquire the necessary cheerfulness and self-control and did it only gradually."[2]

We don't grow easily into maturity. Most of us get dragged into character formation kicking and screaming, because character growth usually occurs by means of persevering through difficult times (see Romans 5:3–5; James 1:2–4). It's often the most unpleasant parts of family life that foster the greatest work in our hearts. Difficult times alone don't guarantee character growth, of course, but if we embrace them with the right attitude and with hearts surrendered to God, they can certainly scour our souls in ways happiness and affluence can't.

As a parent, then, I must learn to appreciate even the hard things about raising a family. I may not *enjoy* the constant cleanup, waking up late at night, giving up something I want to do in order to go on an outing with the whole family, or struggling to resolve the tenth dispute in less than two hours' time between three children—but as a Christian called to die *daily*, I can certainly appreciate and respect these "cross appointments." I don't resent them like I once did; I recognize their place and their role in my life.

For instance, I used to become irritated when the kids opened a new tube of toothpaste before emptying the old one. As soon as the container was four-fifths completed, out came the brand-new, fully bloated tube of Colgate. That left *me* to squeeze the last few helpings onto my toothbrush for another couple weeks. I tried to put the new tube away so the kids would have to use the old one—but invariably they'd find it or, even worse, open yet a third tube!

It finally dawned on me. Kids' thumbs aren't as strong as Daddy's thumbs. It really was a pain for Allison, Graham, and Kelsey to unroll the tube and reroll it with a bit more force, just so they could get another twenty-five cents' worth of toothpaste out of the tube. And I finally saw this as one of the ways I could serve my family.

Such a small and trivial occurrence—but I'm sure most parents could come up with a dozen similar stories without even trying. It's the combined weight of these small events that weigh down our souls. Notice, it wasn't just that Mrs. Moore asked Lewis to make a grocery store visit, or that she asked him to deliver a message, or that she chided him for not walking the dog—it was the *combined pressure* that caused such angst.

That's what family life does. Little irritations build on each other until they become larger than any of us could have imagined. If you had told me as an eighteen-year-old that I'd eventually resent my kids for not draining the toothpaste tube, I would have told you, "I'll never be that petty." But I wouldn't have realized as an eighteen-year-old that it's never *just* the toothpaste; it's everything surrounding the toothpaste that sets us off. The toothpaste is just the trigger, not the ammunition.

That's why we sometimes need to rethink those things that really "annoy" us, and then see if the problem isn't really *our annoyance*. Maybe we're being selfish. Maybe we're being unrealistic. Maybe we're being uncharitable. Maybe we've allowed bitterness to build up to such an extent that something really small suddenly becomes very large. In any case, instead of focusing on changing and lecturing our kids over these issues, perhaps we should really think about changing *ourselves*.

The reason family life so excels in bringing up these issues is that the very act of actually living with someone guarantees rubbing up against each other, having to serve each other, and being put out by each other—all of which require us to die to self; hence my earlier phrase, *cross appointments*.

Modern movies and romance novels look at romance as the place where we will truly live out all our unrealistic expectations: unconditional love, constant encouragement, unflagging affection, roaring romance, and perpetual appreciation. But family life is real, and from a Christian perspective, family life is the place where I learn to *die*—to my own selfish desires, my addiction to comfort, my pride, and my sense of entitlement.

I value family life in part because it so frequently points me to the cross—God's provision for my sin and my family's sin, and God's metaphor for me to die to myself *on a daily basis*. Any situation that so readily reminds me of my calling—to live by the gospel—takes on transcendent importance in my life. It gives me a context to value not just the laughter but also the grueling, rarely appreciated, and often unnoticed acts of service and selflessness.

Maybe you, like me, entered family life with a laundry list of expectations and hopes. This week, consider what God is calling you to die to. What point of selfishness does he want to slay? What resentment is building up in you that needs to be crucified, lest you explode? What character quality is God allowing to be tested? How hot must he allow the heat to grow to before you finally accept your role as a cross-carrying servant?

*Heavenly Father, help us to understand that the very things we often resent most about raising children are the very things that you use to shape our souls. Let us embrace these chastising moments rather than resent them. You are doing a great work in our souls that we don't want to miss out on. In Jesus' name, amen.*

## Questions for Reflection

1. Have you ever felt like C. S. Lewis did—about to explode with exasperation because of the duties of family life? How can you learn to embrace these moments rather than resent them?

2. What's your equivalent of "a tube of toothpaste"— something your family does that bothers you, even though you know the real problem is that you let it annoy you instead of embracing it as a way to serve your family? Are you willing to surrender your resentment?

**33**

# YOU COMPLETE ME

*Let perseverance finish its work so that you may*
*be mature and complete, not lacking anything.*
JAMES 1:4

WHAT'S THE MOST IMPORTANT WORD IN CHRISTIAN THEOLOGY?
I've asked many groups this question, and the answers are usually
pretty similar:

Grace.

Love.

Faith.

Truth.

All good answers, but Elton Trueblood, a well-known writer of the
mid-twentieth century, had a different perspective. He suggests the
most valuable word is the seemingly modest *and*.

So often, we gravitate toward extremes, but God holds up two
truths that at first glance appear to defy human logic: Jesus is fully God
*and* fully human. God is merciful *and* he holds sinners accountable.
God is strong *and* he is gentle. We are holy *and* we are being made holy.

Heresy happens when we forget the *and*.

Kids can help us learn the importance of the *and*, as I found out during a difficult season in my own parenting journey.

One of our kids was having incessant angry outbursts. Confronting this challenge had revealed my own weaknesses as a person. Lisa and I went to an insightful counselor to get a better grip on how to handle this situation. "Gary," the counselor said, "I'm thinking you have a difficult time dealing honestly with your anger about all of this." She went on, "What are you going to do? As soon as this child makes your life miserable for two hours, are you going to slip off into your study and write about gentleness and peace?"

That's when Lisa laughed. "Well, as a matter of fact," Lisa said, "gentleness *is* one of his talks people like most."

God used this child to show me that I was becoming a bit unbalanced, needing to be a bit more forthright and direct in my dealings with this child.

While it is true that gentleness is a key component of who God is—and therefore an indicator of what we should become—it's also true that God wears his gentleness with his strength. Consider these words from Isaiah 40:10–11:

> See, the Sovereign LORD comes with power,
>     and he rules with a mighty arm. . . .
> He tends his flock like a shepherd:
>     He gathers the lambs in his arms
> and carries them close to his heart;
>     he gently leads those that have young.

God can come "with power" while also "gently" leading his lambs. He is not either strong *or* gentle; he is both, simultaneously.

In many ways, kids reveal the places in our lives where we've gravitated toward extremes. We see our sharp edges, our weaknesses, and the convincing evidence that we are not yet fully rounded people. Children point out where we need more work.

God is brilliant at sending us children who work on us in this way. A gruff parent inevitably gets a very sensitive daughter. A book-loving dad watches in horror as his son becomes a sports fanatic. A very refined woman is mortified to learn that her daughter is a tomboy. Along the way, these children unmask our prejudices and uncover our most glaring weaknesses, the areas where we find it most difficult to love, accept, and forgive.

This reality isn't hard to accept if we'll simply admit we're not perfect. In the abstract, such a statement seems so obvious, but in the concrete moment, it can feel painful. So for this week's exercise, repeat after me: "I am not perfect. There are holes in my character and plenty of weaknesses in my personality. And it's guaranteed that my kids will intuitively discern, and consistently reveal, my most glaring faults."

Now watch as God uses your children in the coming days to show you exactly *where* you're not perfect. I suspect you know about many of these areas. But be open to surprises. Expect the process of parenting to put a spotlight on a hidden weakness—and then thank God for providing parenting as a valuable aid for your spiritual growth.

*Heavenly Father, you are the only complete being who holds all his wonderful qualities in perfect balance. Help us to grow in those areas where we camp out in the extremes; open our eyes as you use our children to mature our souls. In Jesus' name, amen.*

## Questions for Reflection

1. Is there a character propensity you tend to exhibit to an extreme—extra gentle or always harsh, controlling or passive, too serious or too flighty? How has parenting revealed this weakness to you?

2. Share where you'd like to grow in order to become more "balanced" in your maturity; pray for each other that God would grant his empowering grace to assist you in this effort.

# 34

# REAL LIFE

*You may have had to suffer grief in all kinds of trials.*
*These have come so that the proven genuineness of*
*your faith—of greater worth than gold, which perishes*
*even though refined by fire—may result in praise,*
*glory and honor when Jesus Christ is revealed.*

1 PETER 1:6–7

MY FRIEND HAD A MOM WITH A LEGENDARY GIVING NATURE.
Kind, generous, eager to serve, hers was the kind of life marked by too
many acts of help to count. As Chip puts it, "How many people have a
delegation from the local post office, the local grocery store, the local
drugstore, and even the local tire store show up at their funeral to say
thanks for the homemade bread and cinnamon rolls?"

When such a "Dorcas" (Acts 9:36) dies, you hope you can give her
the best of send-offs. Unfortunately, real life crashed the MacGregor
funeral service. It all began when the bagpiper got his kilt stuck on the
handle of the coffin. As Chip explained it, "What should have been a
stirring version of 'Scotland the Brave' ended up sounding a bit like a
cat being strangled." And then the lead pallbearer stumbled and *actually fell into the empty grave.* When Chip leaned down to offer his arm

for assistance, the man took one look at him and said, "Sonny, you're going to need some help."

Yet Chip notes that his mom had a great sense of humor and would have laughed louder than anyone at the day's turn of events. What an inheritance Chip has received! Our best-laid plans—the perfect dinner destroyed, the cleaned house messed up, the trip stopped short by a flat tire or feuding children—will regularly collide with real life. What kind of attitude do we want to pass down to our kids? Can we enjoy the humor of living as fallen people in a fallen world, or will we fire our family with resentment when the smallest things go wrong, when a little rain ruins our outdoor plans or our vacation luggage fails to arrive when we do?

I believe it's our duty to model to our kids how to live in a fallen, sinful world where things go wrong. Even better, we can see these turns of events as God's directing providence. Notice how often Jesus seemed to minister almost by "accident." You certainly don't get the impression he and his disciples went through a carefully calibrated schedule: "At 10:00 a.m., you'll preach the Sermon on the Mount; after that, you'll curse the fig tree. But wrap it all up by 1:00, because that's when you're scheduled to meet the woman at the well."

On the contrary, Jesus used storms, hungry crowds, suddenly active demons, and seemingly random wayside meetings to spread his ministry and message.

Anybody can have a good attitude when things go perfectly and nothing goes wrong; what marks a truly Christian family is when they remain calm, gracious, and gentle as real life assaults their best-laid plans. Why? It's at these moments we make our faith seem particularly real to our children. During these seasons, our kids can witness firsthand the blessing of a faith-filled life.

Family life is as real as it gets! Why do kids always seem to get their earaches twenty-four hours before the vacation plane is scheduled to take off? Why do moms get hit with crushing cramps the day they're trying to serve the Thanksgiving dinner? Why do dads get laid off two weeks before Christmas?

Such trials, the Bible tells us, test whether our faith "may be proved genuine." How we accept and respond to these crises reveals to our children the sort of spiritual fiber we really have. If we weather these trials well, our kids may follow our spiritual lead, which will "result in praise, glory and honor when Jesus is revealed."

What's a flat tire compared to *that*?

Over the next seven days, let's ask God to give us gracious hearts, hearts that roll with life's punches, hearts that see humor where others see only frustration—it's one of the richest inheritances we can pass down.

Just ask my friend Chip MacGregor.

*Heavenly Father, your presence is often revealed most*
*clearly when you grant us peace and patience in the midst of*
*disappointment and crisis. Help us focus more on our reactions*
*than on our disappointments. In Jesus' name, amen.*

## Questions for Reflection

1. Talk about the most recent family disappointment—a vacation disaster, a weather-related event, anything unfortunate that caused great concern: how did you (or the two of you) respond to that event? Do you think your kids saw the presence of Christ in your response, or did they see a parent acting without a foundation of faith?

2. The next time such an event occurs, what can you do to remember the truth of 1 Peter 1:6–7, that trials come to prove our faith genuine so that God may be glorified?

# FINGER-POINTING

*"Why do you look at the speck of sawdust in your brother's eye and pay no attention to the plank in your own eye? How can you say to your brother, 'Brother, let me take the speck out of your eye,' when you yourself fail to see the plank in your own eye? You hypocrite, first take the plank out of your eye, and then you will see clearly to remove the speck from your brother's eye."*

LUKE 6:41–42

RELIGION PROFESSOR JERRY SITTSER CAPTURES ONE OF FAMILY life's most fundamental spiritual problems: finger-pointing.

Most homes are like mine, single parent or not. They seem to follow a similar pattern. Family members use the misbehavior of each other to excuse their own. A wife whines, "My husband is never home on time." Her husband responds, "She's such a crab when I'm home that it makes me want to stay away." A brother accuses a sister, "She comes into my room all the time without asking." She counters, "He's always taking my CDs. I can get them if I want to. They're mine."[1]

What can break us out of this spiritual morass? If everybody always blames someone else, how can fault ever be determined? How can the home life ever change?

Instead of offering a three-step resolution process, in the verse above Jesus prescribes the spiritual virtue of *humility*. Humility is the only antidote, the only medicine strong enough to take a household filled with blame and backbiting and turn it into a place of growth and encouragement.

But here's the tricky part: Jerry Sittser would tell us that the first person, the primary patient, the student most in need of this lesson is the *parent*. We need to take the lead and set the example. Jerry made this observation:

> As long as no one is willing to change first, then nothing will ever change. Few people dare to look at themselves as critically as they view others. We demand that the world change according to our wishes. We even pray for it. . . .
>
> We need to pray for ourselves too, asking that God change us, whether or not he chooses to change the world around us. We need to ask God to take this fragile, selfish, flawed self of ours and make it more like him. God will answer that prayer. It is a prayer that makes his heart glad.[2]

In one sense, family life is no respecter of persons. By virtue of our position as parents, we have authority over our children—but under the cross we all stand on level ground. Our little plot of earth isn't even a centimeter higher than that of a newborn baby—we remain just as in need of God's grace, and we require equal amounts of spiritual transformation.

Imagine the tone we could set in our homes if our children heard their mothers or fathers say, "The way I lost my temper this morning was wrong. God has convicted me that I acted in a sinful manner. I'm so sorry that you had to bear the brunt of my sinful reaction, and I thank God he has given me a family like this one where I can learn these valuable lessons. Please forgive me. I don't want to respond in this way in the future."

Suddenly, the kids won't feel like they're the only ones always being challenged. They'll understand that God is at work on all of us, and they'll be far more likely to admit, "Well, we're sorry we were squabbling so much; that must really have been irritating."

On the heels of this experience, when we talk to our daughter or son about "trespassing" into a sibling's bedroom or "stealing" CDs, they'll have seen repentance modeled. They'll have witnessed a Christian receiving conviction from God and then asking for forgiveness. They'll have learned how to question their own hearts.

But if they never see their parents do this—if they only see their parents pointing out their children's faults—where will they learn how to challenge themselves? It certainly won't come naturally. Learning to question ourselves is about the most difficult experience in life. It is graduate school spirituality. If humility does not get purposefully taught and consistently modeled, our kids will never get it.

Apart from pointing our children to faith in Jesus, this willingness to question ourselves may be one of the most valuable lessons we can impart to our children. Without this humble practice, fighting and dissension will *never* cease. During most disputes, it's not just one kid who's in the wrong; *both* have usually sinned—and each one tries to use the other's sin as his or her excuse to sin. It is futile to try to resolve such a dispute until each child becomes willing to acknowledge his or her own shortcomings. Only when we admit our own sin and take responsibility for that sin can we live in peace and harmony.

I am still on this journey. Sin is an ever-present reality in our house; expecting one lesson on the theology of sin to change the climate is like spitting into the desert and declaring the drought over. Why? Because sin is as tenacious as it is terrible; it won't just "go away." It has to be continuously crucified, which means we must model humility again and again and again.

The older I get as a parent, the less faith I put in trite how-to models and the more emphasis I place in examining the spiritual realities—sin, selfishness, pride—and in applying the spiritual remedies—confession, forgiveness, and humility.

*Heavenly Father, help us receive your Son's words and seek to take the plank out of our eye first. Even when others have sinned first, let us be the first to repent wherever we have contributed sin. In Jesus' name, amen.*

## Questions for Reflection

1. What sin of yours is most injurious to your family? When is this sin most likely to be displayed?
2. How can we avoid letting the sin of others lead us into our own sinful response?
3. Discuss the most appropriate way for a parent to model repentance even in the face of an unrepentant child.

# LEADING TO RIGHTEOUSNESS

*Multitudes who sleep in the dust of the earth will
awake: some to everlasting life, others to shame and
everlasting contempt. Those who are wise will shine
like the brightness of the heavens, and those who lead
many to righteousness, like the stars for ever and ever.*

DANIEL 12:2–3

WHILE MANY RELIGIONS TALK ABOUT PERSONAL SPIRITUAL
growth, Christianity stands apart in stressing the glory of helping
*others* grow. In fact, from the world's viewpoint, that's the shame of
Christianity: "Why can't you just leave everybody alone instead of
always trying to convert us?" we are asked.

The answer is simple: the Great Commission (Matthew 28:18–20)
isn't merely about being righteous but about leading others to righteousness. And the words spoken to Daniel emphasize this: those who *lead*
many to righteousness "will shine like . . . the stars for ever and ever."

This call to lead others into holiness provides yet another piece of
evidence for the holiness and high calling of family life, as parenting
offers one of the most influential and effective ways to lead our children
to righteousness. What makes parenting sacred is its God-ordained

purpose and God-ordained aim: he calls us to raise children for the glory of God who will faithfully serve God's kingdom. As we do this, we store up heavenly rewards in which we "will shine like . . . the stars for ever and ever."

Although we have no greater calling or glory than to lead our children to righteousness, many parents feel tempted to focus on much lesser goals. When I was growing up, I knew of a young man about my age whose father had raised him to be an NFL quarterback. Much was made of the fact that his dad had drilled him for years and that the boy had never eaten a Big Mac. He left college early and entered the NFL, only to quickly fizzle out. His father's dream died after it came out that the young man had put worse things than a Big Mac (namely, drugs) into his body. He never came close to reaching his potential as an athlete.

Some mothers want to lead their children to great marriages. Others want to lead their children to fame, so they virtually prostitute their early adolescents to the entertainment industry.

But the Bible calls us to lead our children to *righteousness*. That's the greatest aim we can ever adopt. God calls us to remain focused on their eternal destiny—far more than we should care about their athletic skills, grade point average, musical ability, manners, and social acceptance.

It strikes me that the Bible's description of Barnabas—"He was a good man, full of the Holy Spirit and faith" (Acts 11:24)—gives so little information about him. Was Barnabas a carpenter? A shepherd? A farmer? Were his parents poor or affluent? What color hair did he have? Was he heavy or thin? Did he have a good singing voice? Was he a good athlete?

We don't know—and on this side of eternity, we never will. In the biblical writer's eyes, all of that was superfluous. What mattered most was what we've been told: he had sterling character, he was filled with God's Spirit, and he walked by faith. He was a "good" man—end of story. That's an eternal perspective worth emulating for our own children.

I can't imagine any more painful ordeal than to watch at the great judgment as one of my children steps up to be treated, as Daniel puts it, with "shame and everlasting contempt." On the other hand, I can't imagine a higher joy than to see them "shine like the brightness of the heavens." Imagine the smile such a heavenly commendation will bring to your face, the glory you will share with your children, the joy that will swell your new and pure spiritual heart!

If we lose sight of that judgment day, we risk missing the ultimate purpose of parenting and thus find we've wasted our energy focusing on lesser aims. It's not that we don't care about manners, athletics, grades, and social acceptance; but we remember that our *greatest* call is to lead our children to righteousness. When they stand alone before God, it won't matter how early in life they were potty trained; we won't care whether they could run a mile in four minutes or shoot below par in a round of golf; it won't matter if they earned a six-figure income or died with a six-figure debt or could fit into a size 2 dress. What will matter is that they take their place alongside us in the glorious reality God calls heaven.

Is this your focus today—leading your children to righteousness?

*Heavenly Father, thank you for a word that reminds us of what leads to eternal happiness. Help us to focus on those things in our children for which they will be eternally known and rewarded. In Jesus' name, amen.*

## Questions for Reflection

1. If someone were to consider your past several conversations with each one of your children, what would they conclude is your first concern about the kind of person you want them to become?

2. How can parents practically focus on helping their children become like Barnabas, a "good man [woman], full of the Holy Spirit and faith"?

# REMEMBER YOU'LL
# BE REMEMBERED

*When Jacob had finished giving instructions to his*
*sons, he drew his feet up into the bed, breathed his last*
*and was gathered to his people. Joseph threw himself*
*upon his father and wept over him and kissed him.*

GENESIS 49:33–50:1

HOW MANY MAGAZINE ARTICLES AND BLOG POSTS HAVE ASKED celebrities what they'd like written on their tombstones? Too many to count, that's for sure. But I could care less what someone carves in stone; I'm far more concerned about what gets carved on the hearts of my children.

Sometimes I think it helps to take a step back and remind ourselves that our infants won't always be babies; our toddlers won't always be elementary students; our teens won't always be adolescents. We are influencing future adults, some of whom will remember their parents with casual indifference, some with malicious conflict, and some with passionate gratitude and love.

Donna Isaacson's father was fifty-seven when she was born. He took her hiking, gave her a love for the outdoors, and explained to her his passion for Indian artifacts. Though Donna came relatively late in his life (he was seventy by the time Donna reached her teens), he made room for his daughter and reaped a relationship filled with gratitude and love. I'll let Donna tell the story:

> God gives us things in life we don't always ask for, . . . and sometimes he tests our strength even further. For me, that ultimate test was my father's death. He passed away four years ago at the age of ninety-eight, and there was no consolation in the fact that he had led a long, fulfilling life. If I heard that one more time during his funeral, I thought I would lose it. It didn't matter to me how and when he died; he was gone. The one person on earth who gave me unconditional love was no longer there for me. With his passing, a huge hole was ripped out of my heart, and I plunged into that deep, dark hole with uncontrollable grief.
>
> As my mourning period continued, I went deeper and deeper into that black abyss. For four years, I engaged in a death wish, slowly dying inside. I had no social life. My life consisted of two things: work and sleep. At night, I'd crawl into a cave under the sheets and get into a fetal position, hoping sleep would come and for a few moments I could forget that he was gone, dream that he was still with me. It hurt so badly.[1]

While I hope and pray my children don't descend into a depression like this after I'm gone, I couldn't help but marvel at the pathos of a daughter who misses her father so much that she pined to sleep, only so that she could dream he was still with her.

Thankfully, Donna finally broke out of her stupor when someone pointed out that her father, whom she loved and missed so much, wouldn't want her to suffer this way; to honor him properly, she needed to take her life back, and she did.

Author Gail Waesche Kislevitz faced similar emotions when her mom passed:

> I was still in denial over the death of my mother a few years back; the world I knew ended with her passing. Part of me died with her; I was empty inside, depleted of humor, drive, and ambition. Just getting through the day was a goal. I was desperately trying to learn to live my life without her, and I was failing miserably.[2]

The next time you pick up yet another toy, wash yet another dinner plate or sippy cup, show up for yet another soccer or volleyball game, and you feel tempted to think, "Is this really worth it?" remember that you're going to be remembered. You're laying down an impact that can be so profound that, even if you live to be a hundred years old, your kids won't want to let you go.

Don't take this for granted! As I write this, I'm thinking of a college football coach, who, until recently, had more wins than any other coach in his division. The last several years, though, his program hasn't enjoyed nearly as much success, and every year more and more people are saying he has stayed too long, that he should just get out of the way. In companies across the world, older executives labor under the shadow of the eager ambitions of younger workers who can't wait for the older execs to retire and move on. Aging actors and actresses find their earlier roles increasingly given to younger stars. The world is set up so that one generation quickly replaces the previous one.

But when you go home, you can enjoy being in one of the few places where people genuinely want you to stick around forever.

In most cases, our children are going to grow up and we're going to die. They will then live with memories of our involvement or our absence, our encouragement or our malice, our support or our contempt. As we hold that little five-year-old who just scraped her knee, I guess the question we could ask ourselves is this: What do I want her to be thinking fifty years from now when I'm the one near death and receiving medical care—and she's the one holding my hand to comfort me?

*Heavenly Father, help us to focus today on what we want to be remembered for tomorrow. It's so easy in the day-to-day events to miss the big picture, but let that big picture redirect and refocus our parenting from this point on. In Jesus' name, amen.*

## Questions for Reflection

1. How do you want your kids to remember you when you die? Are you displaying that kind of character and building that kind of relationship now?
2. People today expect the boss to retire, or they want to push the old coach out of the way, but parenting is one relationship where people are eager for the relationship to continue as long as possible. How might that understanding impact what you prioritize today?

# 38

# TAKEN FOR GRANTED

*Praise the LORD, my soul,*
*and forget not all his benefits—*
*who forgives all your sins*
*and heals all your diseases,*
*who redeems your life from the pit*
*and crowns you with love and compassion,*
*who satisfies your desires with good things.*

PSALM 103:2–5

DURING ONE SEASON IN THE LIFE OF ONE OF OUR CHILDREN, we really had to pitch in and remove as much of her stress and the demands on her time as possible. In the course of a child's growing up, every kid will pass through such a season. Maybe it's a difficult academic semester at school. Maybe they're having a particular challenge with a social adjustment. Maybe their hormones are practically boiling inside them and they just need some extra space. When such seasons arise, you know that *now* is the time to lessen the load on their shoulders at home so they can more fully marshal their resources to face the challenge before them.

Many times, this effort goes unnoticed and unappreciated. I remember a mom in Kansas commenting on this with her daughter.

"She has no idea how much I'm doing for her," she said. "No idea! I mean, I'm happy to do it, but she really has no clue."

It struck me that this is exactly how God must feel. Think about it: How many times are we driving down a road, about to carelessly slip into an accident, when God's providence spares us a potentially fatal encounter? We drive on our way with only a momentary glance backward, not realizing God has miraculously intervened.

How many times has God opened the door for us vocationally, relationally, and otherwise, yet we failed to notice his handiwork? Maybe we passed it off as "networking" or our amazing ability to build friends, not realizing the divine hand that moved human hearts on our behalf.

How many times has God spared us from a vicious storm (or saved us in the midst of it), blessed us with a beautiful day, or whispered some Bible verse or encouragement in our hearts, just when we needed it most?

Have you ever pondered how much time God has spent planning your days, thinking about the person you should marry, what gifts he should unleash in you, and what doors he'll open so you can use those gifts? How much creativity did God spend designing your face, developing your personality, and crafting your disposition?

How many times has he thwarted Satan's temptations and kept you from doing something you would regret for the rest of your life? You may have thought the entire episode was just a "private close call." There may have been nothing private about it at all—you just didn't see the holy spiritual battle going on around you.

How many times has our Lord watched over our children, steered them away from danger, and moved them toward positive friends— situations that to this day we know nothing about? Our kids left home to go to school and other activities, and they came back home; we took it for granted, blissfully unaware of how God shepherded them back into our arms.

How many times has God inspired a pastor, a writer, a radio preacher, or a friend to share a message, a Bible verse, or an insight exactly when you needed to hear it? How frequently has God put food on your table and clothes on your frame? Think of how many times you almost had a sharp object poke you in the eye or something drop on your head; or how many times you narrowly escaped falling from a high place. Think it was an accident that you were spared?

God is a busy God. He is pervasively present in our lives, showering us with his goodness and mercy and favor. But how frequently do we specifically recognize what he does for us?

Not nearly often enough.

Some of you may be thinking, "But God *didn't* steer my daughter away from trouble; she's living with her boyfriend!" or, "That hurricane not only hit; it leveled my house!" or, "I've been unemployed for nine months; don't even begin to tell me God has opened doors."

Our culture has the mistaken (and rather modern) notion that when God gets involved, things become *easier*. The ancients understood that when God steps into the fray, things may actually become more difficult—but ultimately more meaningful and character producing. Just because we don't understand the way God moves doesn't mean he has stopped moving; it just means we're too finite to understand his perfect, sovereign ways.

The next time you become aware that your kids aren't noticing how much you do for them, turn that around and remind yourself of how much God does for you! Let's use our children's taking us for granted as a call to worship the God we've likewise been so prone to forget to thank.

*Heavenly Father, forgive us for not giving you the thanks you deserve. It is so wonderful to know that you are actively involved in our lives, even when we don't appreciate it. Thank you, dear Father. In Jesus' name, amen.*

## Questions for Reflection

1. Do you feel appreciated by your children? Do you think they realize just how much you do for them?

2. How can the unseen and often unappreciated sacrifices and service of parenting help us to become more active and avid worshipers of God?

# 39

# TREAT 'EM LIKE GRANDKIDS

*Six days you shall labor and do all your work,*
*but the seventh day is a sabbath to the LORD*
*your God. On it you shall not do any work,*
*neither you, nor your son or daughter.*

DEUTERONOMY 5:13–14

A GRANDFATHER IN YONA ZELDIS MCDONOUGH'S NOVEL *THE FOUR Temperaments* reflects on having grandchildren:

People always said you enjoyed your grandchildren more than you did your children. It was true. When the boys were little, Oscar was still so consumed by anxiety about his career, still plotting and working to shape the trajectory it would take. Looking back, he saw himself as constantly worried: about money, about his music, about Ruth's happiness, about his own. Not that he ignored or neglected his boys; quite the contrary, they were a large part of his thinking and activity. But they were also a part of his worry, woven tightly into the scratchy fabric of his anxiety. He worried about where they went to school, their musical education, their choices in friends and girls, their various annoying or alarming habits. Accidents, choking, drowning, drugs, cigarettes—the worries, no less troubling for their being so common, shared by so many parents. With Isobel [his granddaughter], however, he discovered that he was much less worried. He had no program for her, no agenda. Instead, he was able to live in the present with her much more fully than he could with his own children. And, to his surprise, he was happy there.[1]

One reason grandparents enjoy their grandkids so much is that they're not always trying to fix them or correct them. They take the time to *enjoy* them, and that makes all the difference. They live in the present, with no resentment about the past and less obsession about the future.

In his classic book *Pensees*, Blaise Pascal gave this wise counsel:

Let each of us examine his thoughts; he will find them wholly concerned with the past or the future. We almost never think of the present, and if we do think of it, it is only to see what light it throws on our plans for the future. The present is never our end. The past and the present are our means, the future alone our end. Thus we never actually live, but hope to live, and since we are always planning how to be happy, it is inevitable that we should never be so.[2]

Why is it that when our kids are young, we can't just sit back and enjoy the here and now? To forget about how small our house is, how frustrating the job is, how expensive everything is—and just, for once, to enjoy the moment, making it last by savoring each minute of the day? Why do we spend hours as though they were in limitless supply rather than the very finite number they are, each one bringing the day of our children's departure from home ever closer, bit by bit by bit?

I returned to northern Virginia for a speaking engagement. Two of our children were born in Virginia, and one year, we took a Christmas picture on the Manassas battlefield, with the three children seated at the end of a stone bridge. At the time, they were seven, five, and two years old. Lisa has that picture somewhere in the house; I've seen it many times.

As I walked alone by that bridge almost ten years later, I sat where our kids sat, and I'm somewhat embarrassed to say I cried. I'm not a big crier—my son is fourteen now, and he says he doesn't know if he's ever seen me cry—but I couldn't stop the tears on this occasion. I thought of the decade that had passed and how much my kids mean to me, and yet how fast time is flying by. I thought of the lost weekends, the wasted evenings, the times when I acted like my kids would always be young and would always be with us, and I mourned the loss of each moment I had so carelessly allowed to slip by.

I walked away from that bridge determined to live in the present, eager to capture each moment God gives us, now fully aware and acutely sensitive of how very valuable the present is.

If we lived more in the present, we might not be so utilitarian in our attitudes. So much of parenting is taken up by correcting grammatical mistakes, taxiing the kids back and forth, cleaning the counters, vacuuming the floors, making sure homework gets done. Here's the danger of this approach: when kids feel always under review, always a work in progress, always on their guard, they start to feel like projects instead of deeply loved and accepted children.

In the same way that a body has to be nourished before it can be exercised, so a relationship must be nurtured before it can withstand rebuke, correction, and instruction. Some parents focus so much on what needs to change that they neglect to pause and enjoy what is good and healthy. At times we need to take a step back and rebuild the relationship by going out for a cup of coffee and talking about a topic that won't cause a fight, watching a movie together, playing a game, rooting for our favorite team—whatever it takes to live in the present.

Every now and then, I want to be a grandparent, setting aside certain occasions when I'm just going to enjoy these children—sort of a spiritual Sabbath where I won't do the "work" of parenting but rather just rest and enjoy them. I'm not going to tell them to sit up. I won't bug them about their grammar or ask them if their rooms are clean. Instead, I'll recognize the treasure we call time, the gift of living in the present, the spiritual joy of walking in Sabbath.

One afternoon or evening this week, why don't you join me and do the same? Treat yourself and your kids to a parenting "Sabbath" in which you live fully in the present moment, leaving future anxieties and concerns in God's hands and drinking deeply of the joy of living for the here and now.

*Heavenly Father, help us to appreciate the wonder of the present the way we will someday when active parenting is a distant memory. In the midst of training our kids, help us to enjoy them and embrace the treasure of an ordinary day. In Jesus' name, amen.*

## Questions for Reflection

1. Talk about the difference between grandparenting and parenting; see if there are any insights in that discussion about how you could increase the joy of parenting by taking on the attitude of a grandparent from time to time.

2. How far away are you from being an "empty nester"? Let the reality that parenting is a finite season help you treasure every day with your children as the gift that it is.

# 40

# FOR THE KIDS

*"For I hate divorce!" says the LORD, the God of Israel.*
MALACHI 2:16 NLT

DIVORCE DEVASTATES CHILDREN.

It's time we admit it. I'm tired of hearing about how "the children will learn to cope," or "in the end it will all be for the best," or "given the circumstances, there was nothing else we could do." The Bible allows divorce only for rare circumstances, including adultery and abandonment by a nonbelieving spouse. Other situations exist when a separation probably is in order. Certainly, children must be protected from physical violence and a drug-addicted parent. But except for these rare exceptions, one of our first duties is to hold our marriages together when children are involved. At the very least, we need to admit the great harm we cause to our children when we allow our marriages to fail. Denial is a poor foundation on which to build a new life.

Author Jen Abbas wrote:

> As I entered adulthood . . . , I was stunned to discover that my parents' divorces seemed to affect me *more* each year, not less. . . . When they divorced, they may have thought they made a clean break, but we are

the splintered remains of their parting. Regardless of *why* our parents divorced, the fact remains that their divorce hurt us.[1]

Jen made it very clear: you may be able to give your kids a dozen different reasons why you're seeking a divorce, but in the end, the divorce will *still* hurt enormously. Your reasons will never erase their pain.

Jen explained why: "Divorce alters our identities. It clouds the lens through which we understand the world. It weakens the foundation of our emotional development."[2] In fact, Jen believes "divorce is often *the* defining event of our life, . . . the Achilles' heel to our well-being."[3]

I think about all I want my children to be defined by, all I hope they will remember. How tragic that the one event they might use to describe their childhood, more than any other, would be for their parents to say, "We are going to break up this family."

Researcher Judith Wallerstein points out that divorce is the only crisis where parents put their own wants before their children's needs. "In the crisis of divorce, mothers and fathers put children on hold, attending to adult problems first."[4] And then they tend to exacerbate their children's pain by faulting the children for not "getting over it" or insisting that the children even welcome the person who broke their family apart. One young man laments, "I hated my stepmom because she was the one who broke up my family. And yet I had to visit and eat turkey and mashed potatoes with her and always treat her as if she were an old friend of the family."

Do you see the awkward, morally reprehensible situations we put our kids in when the marriage breaks down? Jen Abbas reflected on such situations: "Oddly enough, it was often *our* failure to accept such changes that marked us as truly troubled. But why shouldn't we be troubled by the breakup of our homes?"[5]

One young woman who was forced to give up weekends and

vacations with her friends so that she could spend time with her non-custodial father expressed her frustration this way: "He did the crime, and I have to pay."[6]

Jen stressed that being older when the divorce occurs doesn't help:

> Imagine you are putting together a puzzle and have only a few pieces left when someone comes in and knocks over the table, scattering all the pieces to the floor. Does the fact that you were almost done lessen the frustration you feel over having to start over? The pain of those who experience parental divorce when they are adults is often down-played. The truth is that divorce still has a major effect because, as you start to reassemble your work, you find that the picture you have been studying has changed.[7]

Whereas those of us who grew up in healthy and intact families view home as a place where we were nurtured and returned to lick our wounds, for children of divorce, said Jen, "home is more likely to be the place where our most serious emotional wounds were inflicted."[8]

Because of what I've read about and discovered in talking to children from divorced homes, I would do just about anything to hold my marriage together—for the kids' sakes, if nothing else. Unless I were married to a truly heinous spouse, whose mere presence terribly damaged my children's spiritual, emotional, and physical health, I would consider it my duty as a parent to bear up under even a very difficult or lonely marriage. (And this is not to judge those of you who made the sometimes courageous decision to stand up to and protect your kids from a destructive spouse.)

Please understand, if you're already divorced, it is not my intention to pick at old wounds. Jesus Christ offers complete forgiveness. Even so, for your own spiritual health, you need to be honest about what your actions have done to your children, seek their forgiveness, and cooperate with God to ease their way. Denying what you've put them through won't make them hurt any less, but admitting your fault may make it easier for them to deal with it in the future.

My real purpose is to address those parents who even now are contemplating breaking up their family or who are putting their families at risk with behavior that threatens their marriages. You may be drifting into an inappropriate relationship, or maybe you've just stopped caring about your marriage and no longer nurture it. I want you to be brutally honest with yourself. In fact, I challenge you to read Jen Abbas's book, *Generation Ex*, and ask yourself, "Am I really willing to do something that devastating to my children? Do I honestly believe my pain is so great it will require inflicting this much agony on my children?" Because what divorce really does is transfer the pain of a parent's difficult marriage onto the shoulders of a child.

Jesus sacrificed himself; he bore our pain and our punishment. As our model, Jesus teaches us to bear our children's pain, not inflict it. We are to carry the cross for our families, not build one that we attach to their shoulders. So many times, I've heard parents say, "I'd take a bullet for my child." Well, if you're in a difficult marriage on the brink of a divorce, here's your chance. To continue with the divorce is essentially to say, "I might be willing to die for my children, but I'm *not* willing to live for them. I won't put up with this situation on their behalf."

That's why this week's application is to leave our children long enough to work on our marriages. I'm talking about getting out together and nurturing that all-important relationship. Once I realize how devastating divorce is, I'm going to make a second, third, and even hundredth effort to keep my marriage strong. The stakes are too high to get lackadaisical. You chose the person with whom you bore these kids; for their sakes, *make it work*.

If you're a young mom who can't bear to leave your child for an hour or two, or if you find yourself ignoring your spouse while you pour all your energies into this tiny bundle of joy, realize that your neglect of your spouse is putting that bundle of joy in grave danger of serious emotional wounds ten years down the road. For your child's sake, if nothing else, spend time loving your husband. Don't allow your emotional, spiritual, or sexual relationship to grow cold.

If you're a man who's getting into compromising situations, who has stopped pursuing his wife and is beginning to look elsewhere, go home one night and take a peek into your kids' bedrooms. Consider how vulnerable their tiny bodies are, and multiply that by a hundred to ascertain their emotional vulnerability. You'll then have a better idea of how dangerous your actions are to their overall well-being. If you wreck your marriage, you will inflict a devastating wound on these children.

Please, don't let the marriage die. Don't even let it grow lukewarm. Certainly, every marriage goes through difficult and lonely seasons; you can't prevent that. But remove the word *divorce* from your vocabulary. Divorce, in most cases, isn't a solution; it creates the family's biggest problem and leads to a whole host of other hurts and trials.

At any rate, let's finally admit it: divorce devastates our children. We have an obligation to do all we can to spare our children from an all-too-common hurt.

*Heavenly Father, you've given us an amazing love for our children. We*
*want to protect them from what could be one of their biggest hurts,*
*so please renew our marriage, grow our relationship with each other,*
*and keep us from ever pursuing a divorce. In Jesus' name, amen.*

## Questions for Reflection

1. How healthy do you believe your marriage is right now? Talk about how each of you is feeling: Lonely? Neglected? Is one of you too busy? Have an honest discussion about the state of your relationship.
2. How can knowing how destructive divorce is to children motivate the two of you to work on these issues and strengthen your marriage?

# THE GREAT PURSUIT

*Dear friends, let us love one another, for love comes
from God. Everyone who loves has been born of God
and knows God. Whoever does not love does not know
God, because God is love. This is how God showed his
love among us: He sent his one and only Son into the
world that we might live through him. This is love: not
that we loved God, but that he loved us and sent his
Son as an atoning sacrifice for our sins. Dear friends,
since God so loved us, we also ought to love one another.
No one has ever seen God; but if we love one another,
God lives in us and his love is made complete in us.*

1 JOHN 4:7–12

"HOW'D YOUR DAY GO?"

"Fine."

"Anything important happen?"

"Not really."

Similar conversations take place every day in SUVs and kitchens all
across the country. What many of us don't realize—particularly those
of us who give up too easily—is that we model our heavenly Father's

love for us when we *pursue* our children. I don't want my kids to think I *tolerate* them or *endure* them. I want them to remember that I pursued them, in part because that's the nature of the love with which God has loved me. "We love each other because he loved us first" (1 John 4:19 NLT).

While we were yet in our sins, God pursued us (Romans 5:8, 10). He took the initiative; he made the effort: "God showed how much he loved us by sending his one and only Son into the world so that we might have eternal life through him" (1 John 4:9 NLT).

Without this notion of initiating love, it's easy to let parenting slip into what we *don't* do: I don't beat my children, I don't yell at them, I don't come home drunk, I don't swear in front of them, and so forth. But love works by a much more proactive policy. Love is a long hug. Love is taking time to talk. Love seeks the other. Love goes on the offensive. It takes action: "This is how we know what love is: Jesus Christ laid down his life for us" (1 John 3:16).

This is one of the greatest challenges for me personally. I get so busy. As a family, we have so many practical things to get done—replacing the light bulbs, paying the mortgage, buying milk, getting the oil changed, fixing dinner, doing the laundry. If we're not careful, these tasks can bury the ultimate purpose behind having a family. And some days I realize, *You know, I don't have a clue what my daughter is feeling as she walks through the hallways of her high school. I couldn't tell you what my son's greatest spiritual challenge is right now. I don't know what Kelsey has been doing in her devotions lately—or even if she's having them.*

It's a slow drift into a lack of vigilance. There are no signs, no monumental turnings—just a gradual falling away from engagement until I wake up one day and realize I'm out of touch. If I don't pursue my kids, I'm not truly parenting them—I'm just feeding and housing them. If I'm not counseling them, enjoying them, and praying for them, I'm more of a hall monitor than a father.

How can I pray if I don't know their biggest fears? Their greatest relational challenges? How they're doing with God? These issues usually don't come up unless we go after them. It's not enough to simply attend sporting events or to know their favorite color or pizza toppings—to fully parent them, we have to break through to the spiritual realities of their everyday lives.

Marriage can be called the great journey, but I think parenting is more accurately called "the great pursuit." It's a mission of love, which requires interest, effort, and initiative. It's the way God loves us, and it's the way we're to love our children.

This week, let's pursue our kids with the same dogged determination God displays in pursuing us.

*Heavenly Father, thank you for loving us so much and cherishing us so much that you choose to be a pursuing God. You never grow weary of getting to know us and following after us. Build in us that same attitude, commitment, and mind-set for our children. In Jesus' name, amen.*

## Questions for Reflection

1. Have you ever had a season in life when you could "feel" how God was pursuing you? Maybe you were lukewarm, but he found a way to break into your heart and win you over with his love. Describe what that felt like, and how it has impacted the way you look at God.

2. Can you answer the most basic questions about your kids' spiritual lives? What are their current biggest fears? Their biggest temptations? Are they aware of their spiritual gifts? How about taking a week to find out the answer to these questions and more?

3. What one or two things do you need to do to initiate more of a "pursuing love" in parenting?

# 42

# POINTING TOWARD
# THE STABLE

*So [the shepherds] hurried off and found Mary
and Joseph, and the baby, who was lying in the
manger. When they had seen him, they spread
the word concerning what had been told them
about this child, and all who heard it were
amazed at what the shepherds said to them.*

LUKE 2:16–18

A CHRISTMAS PROGRAM MOVED ME TO TEARS WHEN DANCE
after dance centered the audience's attention on the newly born Christ
child. These dancers (my two daughters among them) were beautiful and gifted and graceful, but their most significant act occurred
at the end, when, through their motions and the stage lighting, they
turned all eyes away from themselves and toward the feeding trough—
symbolically, toward *Jesus.*

It was a splendid ending, and though Christmas comes just once
a year, its penetrating truth should pierce our hearts every second of
every day: we live to point others to Jesus.

This purpose—living to point others to Jesus—is essential to the notion of sacred parenting. When parenting is about *me*—my comfort, my fulfillment, my happiness, my joy in life, whatever—I'll regularly compare the cost with the personal benefit. But when I live to point others to Jesus, personal sacrifice is a red carpet leading them to the place I desire them to go to above all else.

The glorious day will come when nothing else will matter but him. Forgiving and being forgiven—that will all be over. Measuring our perceived wants against faithful stewardship of the resources God has given us—that'll be in the past. Paying bills, scheduling doctor and dentist visits, attending sporting events and school programs—nothing but history. In one incredible, all-consuming moment, every eye of every human who ever lived will be riveted by the splendor of God's glory.

Pointing others to Jesus is the guiding principle and motivation of sacred parenting. When we consider our children's activities, their friendships, the neighborhoods we live in, potential moves we might make, our children's use of free time, how to educate them—the root issue is how this decision will ultimately affect their relationship with the child born in Bethlehem two thousand years ago.

Yeah, they may improve as a gymnast if they leave home and train with that internationally renowned instructor—but how will it affect their love for the Lord and their training in him? Yeah, that school may have certain educational advantages—but how does that weigh with crafting a heart captured by its affection for Jesus?

This purpose influences not only how we parent our children; it also sheds light on our own sacrifices. I can lose this focus a dozen times or more in a single day. But I know I'm a much better parent when this vision—pointing others toward Jesus—drives me, when it so consumes me that I don't see anything else. My own sacrifice?

What's that compared to the cross? The financial cost? Just how much is heaven worth? One more obligation on my time? Hey, I've got eternity waiting for me!

But without this vision, I can act like a martyr for giving up thirty minutes of television. I can make postponing the purchase of a new set of golf clubs the equivalent of giving up everything I have to the poor. I can make a busy day running errands seem like it's half my life.

This day, let's turn our heads, our hearts, our minds, our souls— our entire being—toward that little baby who grew up to reveal himself as Savior and King. Are our kids living to point others toward him? Are we living to point others toward him? Or are our families being distracted with selfish aims and selfish ambition?

I've told my kids, "*Our* story is built on *his* story." Our family life is there to point to the "First Family"—Mary and Joseph and Jesus. In the ultimate scheme of things, *we* don't matter. This may sound harsh in this self-actualizing age, but the truth is, if I had never existed, this world wouldn't be substantially different. But Jesus is *all*. Without him, there would be nothing. He is the focal point of eternity, and our calling is to take whatever tiny little light he's given us and point it straight into his overwhelming glory.

To parent is to proclaim the glory of God—his worth, his wonder, his majesty. Is your family focused on pointing others toward him?

*Heavenly Father, when you sent your Son, you sent our hope, our joy, and*
*our salvation. Let us remember that family life isn't about us as much*
*as it is about pointing others to your Son. In his name we pray, amen.*

## Questions for Reflection

1. Do you think your personal life is bent toward "pointing others to Jesus" or do your actions and focus reveal a different aim? How do you feel about that?

2. What current parenting decisions do you need to make that might be impacted when you remind yourself that parenting is about pointing others to Jesus?

# 43

# IMMORTALS IN OUR HOUSE

*Very truly I tell you, whoever believes in me will do the works I have been doing, and they will do even greater things than these, because I am going to the Father.*

JOHN 14:12

FOR CENTURIES, JEWISH MOTHERS EAGERLY ANTICIPATED THE birth of a child, because each one asked one of two questions: "Will this boy grow up to become the Messiah?" or, "Will this daughter become the mother of the Anointed One?"

Christians believe these questions have been definitively answered, but every birth is still filled with enormous promise, more than most of us realize. A famous schoolmaster in Britain became well-known for his practice of doffing his hat to his students. When asked why, he replied, "I never know which boy may grow up to be prime minister one day."

This principle is even truer spiritually than it is politically. Jesus made one of his most astonishing statements in preparing his disciples for his death and departure: "Very truly I tell you, whoever believes in me will do the works I have been doing, and they will do even greater things than these, because I am going to the Father" (John 14:12).

My son isn't the Messiah. Neither of my daughters will give birth to the Anointed One. But according to the Messiah, all three can do even greater things than the Messiah did, because the Messiah has sent his Holy Spirit to guide and empower them.

When you look at a drooling baby, a toddler with spaghetti sauce on her shirt, a preteen who hasn't changed his socks for five days, or a teen with enough pimples to play "connect the dots" on her face, it's easy to forget we are raising, in C. S. Lewis's words, immortals—men and women who can impact eternity and who will live forever in unimaginable glory and beauty.

Lewis gave this explanation:

> It is a serious thing to . . . remember that the dullest and most uninteresting person you may talk to may one day be a creature which, if you saw it now, you would be strongly tempted to worship. . . . It is in light of these overwhelming possibilities, it is with the awe and the circumspection proper to them, that we should conduct all our dealings with one another, all friendships, all loves, all play, all politics. *There are no ordinary people. You have never talked to a mere mortal.* Nations, cultures, arts, civilization—these are mortal, and their life is to ours as the life of a gnat. But it is immortals whom we joke with, work with, marry, snub, and exploit.[1]

If, in light of eternity, there are no ordinary people, that means there are no ordinary babies, no ordinary toddlers, no ordinary grade-schoolers, and no ordinary teens. You live with a young person who, when inspired and empowered by the Holy Spirit, can do things even greater than the things done by the Messiah himself! And when this Messiah returns, and your son or daughter loses his or her earthly body and assumes the immortal one, he or she will shine like the brightest and purest star you have ever seen.

If we *really* believe in eternity, if we are truly serious about life after death—about reigning with him—then can we ever look at our children in the same way again? You are raising a future king or queen, an immortal regent, a being of incredible, almost unimaginable, potential and worth. Hebrews 11:23 tells us that Moses' parents hid him for three months after he was born "because they saw he was no ordinary child." *Every* parent should recognize that he or she is raising "no ordinary child."

I wonder how much our homes and our attitudes and our perspectives would change if, when we entered our kids' rooms, instead of doffing our hats we took off our shoes, remembering that we are walking on holy ground.

Your home is more than a house; it is a temple of immortals, a holy and sacred place in heaven's sight.

*Lord God, a baby can seem so ordinary, but when that child grows and is empowered by you, she or he can become a powerful force for the work of your heavenly kingdom. Remind us every day of the amazing potential represented by each child we parent. In Jesus' name, amen.*

## Questions for Reflection

1. Talk about each one of your children—their particular gifts, their potential callings, their unique makeup—and imagine what they might become if they fully surrender their hearts and minds to God's Holy Spirit.

2. How can we build a sense of "destiny" in each of our children? How do we help them understand how God wants to use them in a mighty way?

# 44

# OVERWHELMED

*Where is the wise person? Where is the teacher of the*
*law? Where is the philosopher of this age? Has not*
*God made foolish the wisdom of the world? . . . For the*
*foolishness of God is wiser than human wisdom, and*
*the weakness of God is stronger than human strength.*

1 CORINTHIANS 1:20, 25

DO YOU EVER FEEL OVERWHELMED WITH THE DEMANDS AND
skills parenting requires of you?

I hope so.

Johann Christoph Arnold wisely wrote, "Only the adult who stands
like a child before the grace of God is fit to raise a child."[1]

In one of God's most brilliant ironies, he uses the process of raising
children to become adults to help adults become more like children.
Remember, Jesus said we must become like children to enter the kingdom of God. Children often feel overwhelmed, but in our arrogance as
adults, we start to think we have everything figured out—until God in
his mercy sends us children, and we realize how much wisdom, character, patience, understanding, and godliness we lack.

Little children have to ask when they want a drink, when they want to eat, when they want to get out of bed, when they want to play a game. They are always *asking*, aren't they? And God wants *us* to ask as well. He delights in our dependence and relishes our reliance.

Experienced spiritual directors recognize there is a season when a new believer's infatuation with the faith often morphs into arrogance of the faith. At first we feel overwhelmed by all that Christianity is; then one day we wake up and think we have it all figured out and everybody else should just get on board and follow us. We need to pass through this arrogance into a more mature disposition—one referenced by Paul:

> When I came to you, I did not come with eloquence or human wisdom as I proclaimed to you the testimony about God. For I resolved to know nothing while I was with you except Jesus Christ and him crucified. I came to you in weakness with great fear and trembling. (1 Corinthians 2:1–3)

Let's allow our children to lift us up by first taking us down a notch or two. It is spiritually enriching to be humbled, to be reminded of our need for God's power, God's wisdom, God's patience, God's direction, God's provision, and to know that on our own we just don't have what it takes. When we get pushed past the edges of our natural strength, only to fall into the supernatural provision of God's power, then we've come full circle as believers: "My message and my preaching were not with wise and persuasive words, but with a demonstration of the Spirit's power, so that your faith might not rest on human wisdom, but on God's power" (1 Corinthians 2:4–5).

Our natural human pride pushes us into independence and the mind-set that we have it all figured out. This week, let God use your children to place you back into the process of humble listener, questioner, and seeker. Let the myriad demands of parenting remind us that without God's provision, we have no hope. We need to exchange our own wisdom for his.

Have you grown proud? Have you become independent? Do you sometimes pass an entire day, or maybe even a full week, without honestly and earnestly seeking God's infilling power and superior wisdom? When did you last throw yourself before the Lord and confess, "Without you, I have *nothing* to give these children"?

If you can't remember, why not start today?

*Heavenly Father, remind us that humble dependence is a form*
*of worship, an acknowledgement that you want to equip us.*
*We know that the more we are dependent on you, the more*
*we will have an impact on others. In Jesus' name, amen.*

## Questions for Reflection

1. In what way do you think we need to "become like little children," according to Jesus (Matthew 18:3)?
2. Have you ever missed an opportunity or messed something up when you didn't rely on God but thought you could do it on your own? Talk about that.
3. How is parenting helping you learn to be more dependent on God today?

**45**

# SHAMEFUL HAPPINESS

*Their glory is in their shame.*
PHILIPPIANS 3:19

WHEN MY BOOK *SACRED MARRIAGE* RECEIVED THE SUBTITLE "What if God designed marriage to make us holy more than to make us happy?" I never intended to become known as advocating "antihappiness." Nor did I want anyone to believe I see happiness and holiness as mutually exclusive. I don't—and I certainly wish happiness for my children in their own marriages. But our culture has divorced happiness from its original meaning and stripped it of its original nobility until it has been perverted to mean something entirely new and alien.

You can tell a great deal about a person's spiritual health by what makes him or her, as we now define it, *happy*. In fact, I recently read a very sad quote about happiness. An accomplished athlete coupled up with another celebrity following his divorce. While admitting he misses his children, he told a reporter, "I'm in a good, happy place. I've never been happier."

I wonder how this athlete's kids felt knowing their dad is now "happier than he's ever been" since he no longer lives with them, and their mother (whose quotes in the media make clear her sadness) must learn to live without him. How do you think that makes *them* view "happiness"?

If we can be happy while deliberately leaving our children; if we can be happy while deserting a woman who has come to depend on us emotionally and financially and spiritually—then shame on us! I mean it: shame on us! If our *best* feelings come on the backs of our spouse's and children's *worst* feelings, who wants them?

Let's say my marriage did break up—God forbid, but for the sake of argument, let's just say it did. If so, I hope I'd feel miserable. I hope the pain of the separation from my kids would grow so great that I'd move heaven and hell to get my family back together again.

I'd be ashamed of myself if I were happy. I can't even imagine metaphorically slapping my children in the face by saying, "I'm happier now with this new woman than I ever was living with you and your mother." If I could be happy knowing I had participated in the destruction of my children's family, that alone would be evidence enough that I had lost my spiritual core.

Happiness isn't a bad thing; it's a blessed thing. It's not something we should run from or feel ashamed about. But when a man or woman can feel happier destroying their family than living with them, I don't think it's really "happiness" they're experiencing. Certainly, their actions indicate that they value short-term emotional highs over long-term joy and meaning. They place momentary pleasantness over the inner satisfaction that comes from being responsible, loyal, and faithful.

But if happiness really does come from leaving a woman you've built a history with and raised several children with, and then taking up with some new woman you've known for less than a year, *then I don't want it*. If that's what I have to do to get "happy," God forbid I should ever be happy.

What does give me happiness?

Knowing that though the kids may often argue and even complain about each other, when a real challenge arises, they'll remain each other's biggest supporters.

Knowing that though I have disappointed my wife and sinned against her repeatedly, and though I sometimes take her for granted and don't give her the full attention she deserves, she *still* looks forward to me coming home.

Knowing that our children are growing in the Lord, exploring God's place and call in their lives, and seeking to reach out to others.

Knowing that though our story hasn't been a continuously easy or pleasant one, it is still an unbroken story—five people (and one golden retriever) who have stayed together through it all, committed to each other, occasionally sinning against each other and asking forgiveness, waking up in the same house, praying for each other, seeking God together, and building a history I hope will bring glory to God while also bringing security, peace, comfort, and joy to us.

*That's* what I call happiness.

*Heavenly Father, shape our hearts so that we become happiest*
*with the things that make you happy. In Jesus' name, amen.*

## Questions for Reflection

1. What brings you your greatest happiness in life?
2. Do you think you could be happy doing something that made your children miserable? Are your actions reflecting that in this season of your life?

# 46

# COOPERATIVE PARENTING

*He who forms the mountains,*
*who creates the wind,*
*and who reveals his thoughts to mankind,*
*who turns dawn to darkness,*
*and treads on the heights of the earth—*
*the LORD God Almighty is his name.*

AMOS 4:13

HAVE YOU EVER TAKEN A STEP BACK TO CONSIDER HOW ACTIVE God is in the lives of our children? For starters, God begins reaching out to our kids even before we know they exist; he may well be calling them before we've laid an eye on them. Luke tells us that John the Baptist was filled with the Holy Spirit *even before he was born* (Luke 1:15).

Even while our kids are still tucked in their mothers' bellies, God pursues them; he begins calling them to their spiritual homes before they can even speak. He zealously seeks their good, eagerly plans for their salvation, and generously gives them his constant attention and oversight. As parents we can benefit from and cooperate with this ongoing reality.

We have a son gifted in many ways; he has been spiritually sensitive from the time he was young, and his mind's capabilities far exceed my own. But he has suffered from sinus, asthma, and allergy problems his entire life. Recently, he had a pretty bad breathing spell. He's been going through different types of therapies, all attempting to unblock a consistently stuffed-up system, and I think he just felt weary from fighting what feels like a losing battle.

As I prayed one morning, I sensed very strongly that God wanted me to point out to Graham the many ways God has blessed him. His academic abilities really are off the charts; he's a good athlete, he's sensitive—and I could go on, but I don't want to bore you. Yet God has given him this challenge to bear. Graham needs to learn how to accept both challenges and blessings without losing perspective. God is the author of Graham's life; he knows what he's doing, and he isn't callous in what he allows. I needed to remind Graham of this; otherwise, he could become unbalanced in his perspective on bearing this burden and thus become resentful.

After our talk, Graham said, "You know what verse *really* scares me?"

"No. Which one?"

"The one that says, 'To whom much is given, much will be expected' [see Luke 12:48]. I think of all God has given me with my parents and knowing him so young, and it's like, whoa!"

Instead of being bitter about his trial, Graham suddenly felt over-whelmed with God's goodness to him and filled with the knowledge that he needed to respond faithfully.

I'm so grateful this is just one example of the way God wants to be very active in our parenting. He sees into our children's hearts. God will reveal secret fears, silent struggles, and even cloaked dreams. I can't imagine parenting without God's input. It is such a blessing not to merely guess what is happening but instead to have the benefit of listening to the God who knows my children better than they know themselves. It's truly exciting to live out what the disciples experienced in Mark 16:20: "The Lord worked with them."

This is what makes Christian parenting truly Christian: we listen—not just to our children but to God. The discipline of listening still makes some Christians nervous because it can and has been abused. I don't believe in additional revelation; God isn't going to give me a new doctrine the church has never heard. But he frequently helps me to *apply* the revelation we already have. He motivates me to love my wife and children, and he helps me make wiser decisions based on the absolute, authoritative truth of his Word.

I don't hear from God like this every day. I don't even hear from him every time I ask to hear from him. But if I present myself before him, over the course of several months, each one of my children (and my spouse) will be brought to my mind, and I'll gain a sense of my obligation to love them that day. It may be a warning or it may be an encouragement; it may be a creative idea or a new way of looking at things. But in God's good time, he speaks.

I certainly don't want to profess belief in God with my mouth and then parent as though he doesn't exist or live as though God were mute or deaf. We are blessed to know an all-powerful, all-knowing, all-seeing God who is even more concerned about our children's welfare than we are. He passionately concerns himself with our children's spiritual health and will eagerly cooperate with us in raising them.

Take full advantage of this. Create quiet time in your life to hear his voice. Some people hear God best early in the morning, while for others, it's late at night. Some need to be on their knees in prayer; others turn off the radio in the car and tune in to God while they drive. Still others get surprised by God's voice in the shower or while out for a run. A few may even have an eye-opening dream.

In whatever way God speaks to you, *listen.* If you've never experienced this before, simply confess it: "God, I don't know what I'm doing, but I *know* you made me, and I know you want to get through to me, so do whatever you have to do so that I can hear you."

Cooperating with God is truly one of the greatest helps we have as parents. What will he be saying to you this week?

> *Lord God, it gives us great comfort to know you are actively parenting our children; you are passionately committed to their welfare. Open our ears so that we can learn to cooperate with what you are already doing in their lives. In Jesus' name, amen.*

## Questions for Reflection

1. What comfort do you get from the reality that God is actively "parenting" our children, reaching out to them, watching over them and wooing them into his family?
2. Have you ever received a warning from God, an encouragement from God, or an insight from God about what was happening with one of your children? How did you "hear" it?
3. What can you do to be more open to "cooperative" parenting with God instead of doing it on your own?

# 47

# WHAT YOU WERE BORN TO DO

*Is there anything of which one can say,*
*"Look! This is something new"?*
*It was here already, long ago;*
*it was here before our time.*

ECCLESIASTES 1:10

HAS IT EVER OCCURRED TO YOU THAT THE CHALLENGES YOU face as a parent are nearly identical to those faced by parents five hundred years ago? Society has progressed from horses to airplanes, from scrolls to email, and from ale to Starbucks, but we still have to change diapers in the twenty-first century; we still have to deal with late-night vomiting and toddlers' tantrums. A crying infant is no less irritating to our ears than it was to a mother or father five centuries ago.

The struggles you face as a parent, day in and day out, are not unlike what a woman in Germany faced three hundred years ago, a man in France faced in the Middle Ages, and a couple in Egypt faced over two thousand years ago. Your concerns for your kids' futures, your anxiety over their health and well-being, your passion for their good and their happiness, and your weariness over the daily tasks of family life are nothing new. An essay by Martin Luther written in the early sixteenth century reminds me of all this:

Now observe that when that clever harlot, our natural reason (which the pagans followed in trying to be most clever), takes a look at married life, she turns up her nose and says, "Alas, must I rock the baby, wash its diapers, make its bed, smell its stench, stay up nights with it, take care of it when it cries, heal its rashes and sores, and on top of that care for my wife, provide for her, labor at my trade, take care of this and take care of that, do this and do that, endure this and endure that, and whatever else of bitterness and drudgery married life involves? What, should I make such a prisoner of myself? O you poor, wretched fellow, have you taken a wife? Fie, fie upon such wretchedness and bitterness! It is better to remain free and lead a peaceful, carefree life."[1]

Luther brilliantly captures history's (and our current society's) crass view of family life. Isn't it amazing how similar this view is to many portrayals of marriage offered today? Hollywood loves to glorify single living and immoral romance, while portraying married life as bitter and boring and even soul destroying. How many movies portray a faithfully married man and woman with children in a positive light? I remember the time we returned from a movie featuring yet another single parent, and our daughter, Allison (who was quite young at the time), looked up at me and said, "Why don't they ever make a movie about families like ours where the mom and dad like each other and everybody decides to stay together?"

The world has long fought against the nobility of family life because it has long fought against God. The family is God's design, God's creation, and God's idea. It shouldn't surprise us that a world that hates God will hate his idea of how most of us are called to live. Listen to Luther's response:

What then does Christian faith say to this? It opens its eyes, looks upon all these insignificant, distasteful, and despised duties in the Spirit, and is aware that they are all adorned with divine approval as with the costliest gold and jewels. It says, "O God, because I am certain that thou hast created me as a man and hast from my body begotten this child, I also know for a certainty that it meets with thy perfect pleasure. I confess to thee that I am not worthy to rock the little babe or wash its diapers, or to be entrusted with the care of the child and its mother. How is it that I, without any merit, have come to this distinction of being certain that I am serving thy creature and thy most precious will! O how gladly will I do so, though the duties should be even more insignificant and despised. Neither frost nor heat, neither drudgery nor labor, will distress or dissuade me, for I am certain that it is thus pleasing in thy sight."[2]

Luther looks at family life as an institution designed and ordained by no less an artist than God himself. When God created marriage as a lifelong covenant between a man and a woman, he knew full well the drudgery involved—the work, the pressure, the stress, the conflict. Obviously, he must have had a purpose behind us facing all of this. And since he is our Creator, our Master, and our Lord, we accept his design gratefully, in humility, knowing that what he designed for us must, in the end, be the best for us. In other words, we surrender to family life—with its diapers and duties—because it is the life God has designed for the vast majority of us.

When a man changes a diaper, when a mother puts a child to her sore breasts to feed her, this parent is doing what God created him or her to do, what gives God great delight, what faithful believers have been doing for thousands of years. Let others mock us; let others ridicule us! That's a small price to pay when our dutiful service brings a smile to God's face and pleasure to his heart. This is the world as God created it, and living in it rightly brings great joy to him.

Faithful parent, hear me: heaven rejoices in your service and even cheers you on. The world has mocked and will continue to mock our choices and our estate. But we know the God who called us to live as a family, and we are to find our pleasure, our purpose, and our acceptance from *him*.

You are doing what God created you to do. Look Godward, friend, and be strengthened.

*Heavenly Father, from the beginning of this world you created, we have—with much pain, anxiety, and weariness—birthed and raised children. As you sustained prior generations, sustain us, O Lord. Let us receive life as you designed it to be lived. In Jesus' name, amen.*

## Questions for Reflection

1. In what ways do you think parenting is easier today than it was in Luther's time? Are there any ways in which it is harder?

2. Do you ever sense a negative view of the parental lifestyle, such as described by Martin Luther? Do you find yourself asking such questions? How might the understanding that God created us to face these challenges change the way you live through them?

# 48

# DIVINE DISILLUSIONMENT

*Truly my soul finds rest in God.*
PSALM 62:1

DAVE AND DINA HORNE HAVE AN ADORABLE FIVE-YEAR-OLD daughter named Emma. I was speaking at their church one Sunday, and Emma, along with about twenty other kids in the children's choir, started off the service.

Between the two services, I saw Emma lining up to sing for the second service. "You were fantastic, Emma!" I said. "You guys sounded like stars!"

Emma smiled, and without missing a beat, she asked me, "Are you gonna hear the second service too?"

Something in the human heart virtually guarantees that we can never be noticed enough. It's a lust every bit as strong and every bit as destructive as sexual lust—only *this* lust doesn't wait until adolescence to awaken. We're born with this one, and most of us will die with it.

When it's all about me, I can never be noticed enough, appreciated enough, thanked enough, or complimented sufficiently.

That's why I believe God has created a divine disillusionment inherent in family life. If we're honest, most of us will admit we felt disappointed as children in the love our parents gave to us. Even if we had wonderful parents, our hearts' desire is to be adored, loved, and cherished as only God can love us. No sinful mother and father, with human limitations and their own distractions, can love us so thoroughly that this desire will get fully satisfied.

Disappointments add up until we reach adolescence and finally realize, "I'm not going to be loved by these two people as perfectly as I want to be. What I really need is a soul mate—a boyfriend [or girlfriend]—who will love me the way I really want to be loved."

For a while, a soul mate's love may indeed swell our hearts with satisfaction, but in time, that person's love will also be found wanting. It may take months, or it may take years, but eventually, this soul mate—like our parents—will fail to love us like we really want to be loved.

This will lead us to the third and, I hope, final stage of the divine disillusionment process: we'll think, "I'll have a baby and be such a wonderful, fantastic parent that this child will finally love me like I want to be loved."

At least our method is a little less selfish in this latter stage. We realize we have to give in order to get, but at heart it is still narcissistic, self-centered, and demanding, and it still remains unfulfilled for a very simple reason: if our grown parents couldn't love us like we wanted to be loved, and if our twentysomething soul mate failed to love us as we crave to be loved, why in the world would we expect babies or toddlers to be able to love us this way?

I believe God allows us to go through these three stages, as he patiently waits for us to finally throw our contentment and our need to be loved in *his* direction. God waits as we put our hope in our parents—and we get disappointed. God is patient as we place our hope in a romantic attachment—and we become frustrated. God looks on with forbearance as we throw our hope into intimacy with our children—and then we become tired. All the while he waits for us, quietly whispering, "What you're looking for is *me*. I've been here all along. Put your hope in me."

If we don't allow this divine disillusionment to push us in God's direction, we'll usually shoot off into the universe of substitutions. We may contemplate an affair, going back to the soul-mate line of thinking. Or we may place our hope in something beyond relationships—power, prestige, fame, vocational accomplishment, or some political cause.

As parents, we've been through these first three plateaus. God has been patient with us as we looked elsewhere—but now let's turn our attention to him. It's time we realize our delight depends on his favor. Our hearts will feel satisfied *only* with his love. It's time we stop blaming our parents and our spouses and our children for not noticing us enough, loving us enough, complimenting us enough, appreciating us enough, and supporting us enough, and instead ask God's forgiveness for not looking to him for soul satisfaction.

Consider King David, so ignored by his father that he wasn't even initially presented to Samuel as a possible replacement for Saul; so despised by his wife, Michal, that she compared him to a "vulgar fellow" (2 Samuel 6:20); and so ill-treated by his sons that one challenged him for the throne and even attempted to kill him. In the end, David found his rest in God. He said in verse 1 of Psalm 62: "Truly my soul finds rest in God," and in Psalm 63, David beautifully and poetically poured out his devotion to the only one who hadn't disappointed him:

> You, God, are my God,
>    earnestly I seek you;
> I thirst for you,
>    my whole being longs for you,
> in a dry and parched land

where there is no water. . . .
Your love is better than life. . . .
I will be fully satisfied as with the richest of foods; . . .
Because you are my help,
   I sing in the shadow of your wings.
I cling to you;
   your right hand upholds me.

PSALM 63:1, 3, 5, 7–8

When you read the words of David in Psalms 62 and 63, you are reading the words of a *satisfied* man. He sought validation in his parents—and he got ignored. He sought it in his wife—and he was despised. He sought it in his sons—and he was betrayed. He finally sought it in his God, and he found a love he describes as "better than life."

Consider this week whether you've asked your parents, your spouse, or your children to be a God-substitute. Scorn the futility of putting your hope and your soul's desire in other sinful people. Laugh at it, and, like David, turn your affection to the only one who will ever love you as you long to be loved. Then you will be free to focus on loving instead of being loved. You will be armed with the delight that the one who knows you and understands you more fully and deeply than anyone else is the one who is most interested in you and who will always, without fail, be there on your behalf.

If you ask more from your marriage than God designed it to give, it is not your marriage's fault when you become disappointed. If you ask your parents or your children to be what God never designed them to be, it is not your parents' or your children's fault if they fall short of your expectations.

This week, let's release our loved ones from the desperation that comes from spiritual isolation, and instead let's begin building a life of devotion that will free us up to love instead of being chronically disappointed, to encourage instead of nag, to lift others up instead of burying them with our idealistic expectations. Let us find the path of David, who testified, "I will be fully satisfied as with the richest of foods."

*Heavenly Father, today we celebrate the fact that you are enough. You have loved us and will love as no one else ever has or ever will. Let us place our hope and find our happiness in you. In Jesus' name, amen.*

## Questions for Reflection

1. How have you been disappointed in the love you received (or didn't receive) from your parents? Your spouse? Your kids? How can we turn this disappointment into worship of God?

2. If you rewrote Psalm 63 in your own words—celebrating your love for God and your satisfaction with God—what different words or phrases would you use?

# 49

# THE GREAT TRANSFER

*He must become greater; I must become less.*
John 3:30

For reasons I'll not get into here, I've been excessively modest about my body throughout my life. I never feel comfortable with my shirt off, so much so that even my own family does a double take when they see me shirtless. I remember a vacation on the beaches of Hawaii where I took off my shirt, and my youngest daughter said, "Wow, you look *really* white—like someone who's had a fever for three days."

"Yeah, or like someone who's been dead for a week," the other daughter offered.

Intellectually, I know our bodies are God's good handiwork—his creative design made for his glory. Just as I look at the mountains and say, "There is the glory of God," so I should be able to look in a mirror and say the same.

But I don't.

One day, Lisa noticed that our son was exhibiting some of these same overly modest tendencies. Don't get me wrong—biblical modesty is commendable, but *shame* isn't. Without being intentionally critical,

Lisa recounted to me what happened, and we both knew what she was thinking: "We know where *that* came from, don't we?"

I wish I could model something different for my son—but I can't. But there was one thing I could do. I took my son out for a "guys' lunch"—cheesesteak sandwiches, fries, and colas, with no vegetables—and we had a talk.

"Graham, you know all those pictures of Jesus being crucified?"

"Yeah, Dad."

"They're not very historically accurate."

"What do you mean?"

"When the Romans crucified criminals, they stripped them naked."

Graham gasped. He knew where this was leading.

"Unless they treated Jesus differently," I went on, "they stripped him naked too. Maybe they *did* treat him differently, though the Bible doesn't say they did. But if they didn't, your Lord allowed himself to be stripped naked in front of his mom; a few female followers; and a leering, jeering, and lewd crowd who hated him. He took what would be your and my greatest fear, and he bore that on our behalf, because he loves us."

I paused to let this sink in. "Graham, you know your dad has body issues—but your Lord doesn't. He's perfect. And his willingness to do that shows how much he loves you. If you ever doubt his love, just consider the cross."

It was a difficult realization for me as a young father when it dawned on me one day that Graham would grow up to be disappointed with me. I was so large in his eyes when he was a toddler, and even recently, I heard him tell his best buddy, "See, I told you my dad is a holy man."

But I'm a fallen man. Lisa recently said something to me while she was getting out of the car. I answered sarcastically, just a cutting little joke at her expense, and Graham said, "Oh my gosh!" He was shocked, because he doesn't usually hear me speak to his mother like that. I apologized profusely, but the words had been said—and he heard them.

I wish I could be a perfect example for Graham of how to model Christ to the world, but I fall short every day, so part of my task as a parent is to prepare my kids to deal with their disappointment with me—and this means transferring their allegiance from me to God.

Instead of denying my "body issues," I wanted to use them to show Graham his dad's weakness contrasted with his Lord's strength and glory. While it would break and rebreak my heart if Graham rejected me, it would devastate me beyond comprehension if Graham rejected his God.

"I might let you down, Graham," I wanted to say, "but your God won't *ever* do that. Any positive example I leave will be tempered with a few bad examples I hope you forget—but your God is perfect, consistent, never failing, and never disappointing."

Have you ever thought about preparing your kids to deal with their parental disappointments? Have you ever talked to them about how much more capable their heavenly Father is than their earthly father or mother? Have you ever taken the time to begin the inevitable transfer of their allegiances from you to him?

Physically, we train our kids to take care of themselves—to brush their teeth, to shower regularly, even to floss. Educationally, we train them to get a high school and maybe a college degree. Athletically, we train them to achieve the best in their chosen sports. But what about training them spiritually for their inevitable disappointment with us? Why leave them to make that transition on their own? Why not use their growing understanding of our parental limitations to further cement their relationship with God?

Take your weakness—any weakness—and compare it with God's strength. Our greatest wounds can be the very stepping-stones that lead our children to Christ.

*Heavenly Father, our earnest prayer is that our children would receive you in faith and follow you in practice. Prepare them for the times when they are disappointed in us, and use our limitations to magnify your greatness. In Jesus' name, amen.*

## Questions for Reflection

1. Have your kids reached the age at which they are a little disappointed in you or are beginning to perceive some of your weaknesses? How have you dealt with that so far?

2. How can we consciously "transfer" our children's allegiance from thinking we've got everything together to the worship of God, so that they learn to put their highest allegiance in him? Are there any conversations you need to have with any of your kids in the next several days about this?

# 50

# THE TRUTH OF TOLERANCE

*Be patient with everyone.*
1 Thessalonians 5:14

"Gary, I kind of locked the keys in the car."

I put down the phone, ready to drive over and bail Lisa out, but when I went to retrieve another set of keys, I noticed the empty hooks where we keep Lisa's car keys. Apparently, Lisa had lost the last set. I had to go through her coats, her pants, her purse, her shoulder bags—anything I could think of—to find a key so I could get her home.

Lisa is a lastborn, and she does lastborn things. She loses stuff. She "forgets" her purse or leaves her wallet at the store. Just the other day she told me, "You know, I haven't seen my Starbucks credit card in three months, but nobody's used it, so I figure it must be lost at home."

She saw the look of horror on my face.

"No big deal," she said. "It'll turn up."

She saw my look of doubt.

"Someday."

Some things, Lisa never thinks to buy. Take toilet paper, for instance. I came home from a speaking trip one time and discovered that our three bathrooms had a grand total of one-fifth of a roll of toilet paper, which the family members were dutifully passing around until I got home to buy some more.

"You know," I said, "they sell this stuff at the store." But for whatever reason, if I don't buy our toilet paper, we'll never have it.

After a couple decades of marriage, Lisa and I have accepted that some things will never change, because they won't. Lisa's a lastborn; she's not a proactive, type-A firstborn, and I can't expect her to become an entirely different person just because she's married to me. Lisa has learned that I can leave a mess and not even see the mess; it's not deliberate, but it's frustrating all the same.

"This is all very fine, Gary," some readers might be thinking, "but what does this have to do with *parenting*?"

Plenty.

Our youngest daughter once expressed her frustration with one of Lisa's lastborn characteristics. It sounded a little extreme in the moment to tell her, "You know what, Kelsey? That's never going to change, so you may as well get used to it," but there was, nonetheless, a valuable teaching moment. One day Kelsey is going to marry a man, and the day will surely come when she has to learn to live with real disappointment. This disappointment will inconvenience her, frustrate her, at times perplex her, and occasionally even anger her.

How providential, then, that God has given her two imperfect parents who can teach her the value and necessity of tolerance! As my kids get older, I'm more and more aware of my responsibility to prepare them for married life. They probably get tired of hearing it, but I stress how the skills for family life they develop as brother and sister, son and daughter, will come into great use as husband and wife, father and mother. If they don't learn these skills *now*, they're going to have to learn them *then*, and it'll be much easier for them if they can begin marriage with these skills rather than weigh down a future relationship in its early stages.

Tolerance is a key virtue for communal living. I almost hesitate to use the word *tolerance*, as it has been co-opted by many in our culture to justify obscene forms of evil—but the word still has meaning, value, and truth. Family life grows miserable without tolerance and patience.

This week, consider whether you're missing some prime teaching opportunities. How do your kids see you respond to your spouse's limitations or personality quirks? Are they learning that you deal with the frustration by belittling your spouse in front of your kids? By gossiping about him or her to your friends? Or do they see you dealing with it by building up and being gracious where he or she falls short?

A tolerant wife or husband can make the difference between a home where joy and peace reside and a home where the pressure and tension become so thick you get a headache by merely walking through the door.

Let's teach tolerance.

*Heavenly Father, give us your delight in each other so that we can celebrate our differences with enthusiasm and learn to tolerate frustrations with grace, so that our home remains a place of joy and delight rather than frustration and judgment. In Jesus' name, amen.*

## Questions for Reflection

1. What are some of the things you've had to learn to accept about each other, knowing they'll never change? What are some of the things about your children that you think will probably never change?
2. Talk about how you can begin using lessons of tolerance learned while living with imperfect siblings and parents to help prepare your children for marriage.

# 51

# A LITTLE SLICE OF HEAVEN

*When God gives someone wealth and possessions,*
*and the ability to enjoy them, to accept their lot*
*and be happy in their toil—this is a gift of God.*
*They seldom reflect on the days of their life, because*
*God keeps them occupied with gladness of heart.*

ECCLESIASTES 5:19–20

JIM'S STORY IS AS SAD AS IT IS FAMILIAR. HE AND HIS WIFE, Emma, had been married for almost twenty years. Jim grew bored with his wife, his family, and the predictable routines. In a case of abominable timing, he began an affair with a much younger woman just when Emma's mom was diagnosed with cancer. When Emma found out that Jim had used her visits to the hospital as open windows to visit his mistress, and that the mistress in question was still in her twenties, Emma declared the marriage over.

At first, Jim felt relieved by the turn of events. "I feel deeper in love with Jessie after six months than I ever felt with Emma," he said, but of course that all changed within the next eighteen months.

It almost always does.

When Jim started to see Jessie's faults, he dealt with them the same way he had dealt with problems in his first marriage—he sought solace outside the relationship. This time, however, he tried having an "affair" with his ex-wife, Emma! He gave her an expensive gift for her birthday, started telling her how she was the one who had always been there for him, and even tried to talk about the struggles in his second marriage. Emma, to her credit, would have none of this. "You're starting to do to Jessie what you did to me," she told him flatly, "and I won't be a part of it."

Just as painful to Jim were his children's reactions. They were angry at him for breaking up their family. They took their mother's side, and they resented the expectation that they were to spend time with the woman who was at least partially responsible for wrecking their home.

One afternoon, Jim became honest. "I can hardly bear this," he confessed. "Jessie is so young; she makes me feel so old. She's starting to talk about wanting a family, but I'm forty-five! I don't think I can go through the baby stage again. And there's this younger guy at work that she runs with at lunchtime, and it's just horrible. How can I compete with his hair and his energy and his knowing all the current music groups? I put in a Bee Gees CD, and Jessie just laughs at me. Besides all that, I see Emma and realize she really is the woman I've always loved. Yeah, she has her faults—plenty of them—but we had so much together, and I was such a jerk.

"And I can't tell you what it's like to try to have a relationship with a daughter who looks at you with hate in her eyes. She despises me. Every time Jessie so much as touches me, Amanda [the daughter] flinches. Do you have any idea what I'd give to get back what I lost? All I want is what I used to have—to wake up next to Emma, those crow's-feet around her eyes but a face I've loved for two decades, and to walk downstairs to the kitchen and see Amanda eating a bowl of cereal and hearing her say, 'Hi, Dad,' without any accusation or rebellion in her voice. That's it! Nothing special—just the plain old, boring Saturday morning that used to drive me crazy. I'd give everything I have now—I'd even give my right arm—to get all that back."

The routine of family life can hide the daily miracle we enjoy. Just a simple, quiet Saturday morning sounds like a slice of heaven to a man who has lost it all; but to those of us who still wake up in the same house next to the same spouse with the same kids, we can become blind to what a blessing it really is.

I know that if I were to do what Jim did, the time would come when I'd feel exactly as he does. I'd be willing to swim through hot lava to have just one regular morning like I enjoy all the time now. When we're surrounded by this blessing, it's easy to look at the downside— our spouses' wrinkles or morning breath, the fact that one of the kids left the milk out or the refrigerator door open, a teen waking up at noon, but if something were to happen and it all got taken away, our highest wish would be to restore things to just the way they were— spilled milk and all.

In the heat of a newfound and misplaced affection, it's easy to grow bored with or even to despise the wonder of a quiet morning in a stable home with a long history. But wisdom teaches us that our hearts will eventually grow weary of the hot romance and ache for the quieter and much more profound love of family that we left behind.

Every routine Saturday morning is a blessing, a quiet miracle, a little slice of heaven. Enjoy it. Protect it. Thank God for it. And certainly, don't even *think* about throwing it away. Its familiarity may have masked the wonder; but its absence would tear out your heart.

Parenting certainly has its pains. It calls us to sacrifice, it can be exhausting, and it can test us like nothing else. But it is God's will for us, God's gift to us, and in our heart of hearts we know nothing we do will ever matter quite as much as those "boring" Saturday routines.

This morning, I walked upstairs and saw the rest of the family finally getting around to eating breakfast. Graham was home from cross-country practice, eagerly evaluating his high school team's chances in the coming season. Allison was her quiet self, reading the newspaper and wearing her favorite pajamas. Kelsey was lamenting how a bagel had fallen into the pancake batter. Lisa was outside in the sun, moving the sprinkler to a different spot.

Just an ordinary morning in the eyes of most people, but because I'd been working on this book, my appreciation had grown, and I thought, *You know, it really doesn't get much better than this.* I went around the kitchen and touched each child. I tried to take a mental picture, preserving this moment, and I thanked God for this little slice of heaven right here on earth.

*Lord God, awaken us to the wonder of the ordinary, normal day.*
*Remind us that if tragedy struck, we'd give everything we have*
*to enjoy a moment that we currently take for granted. Help us to*
*appreciate rather than resent these routines. In Jesus' name, amen.*

## Questions for Reflection

1. What are some of your favorite things about "routine" family life? If something were to happen that disrupted everything, what would you miss most about what you currently enjoy?

2. What's a more constructive alternative to having an affair when you experience "boredom," or when the routine becomes overly familiar?

# 52

# A PICTURE PROPHECY

*He will turn the hearts of the parents to their children,*
*and the hearts of the children to their parents.*

MALACHI 4:6

THE OLD TESTAMENT BEGINS WITH A FAMILY IN DYSFUNCTION.
In the very first human family, Adam blames his wife, Eve, for their fall
into sin and Cain kills his brother, Abel (Genesis 3–4).

The story of family dysfunction continues almost as a constant
thread: Noah curses his middle son (Genesis 9:24–27); Abraham agrees
to his son's exile (16:6); Lot's daughters commit incest with him (19:30–
38); Jacob and Esau fight for the firstborn blessing (27:1–40); Joseph's
brothers sell him into slavery (37:12–36); and don't even get me started
about David and his family!

Doesn't it astonish you how, even in the Bible, family dysfunction
gets passed down from generation to generation? After all, these are
our spiritual ancestors—and yet, who among us would choose to have
our families turn out like theirs?

But at the end of this grand story, in the very last verse of the Old
Testament, we finally see what God is up to. He is sending a prophet
who will bring our families back together: "He will turn the hearts of

the parents to their children, and the hearts of the children to their parents" (Malachi 4:6).

The story that begins with a broken family ends with the promise of reunited families who have recovered their glory, their purpose, and their fulfillment. Admittedly, there's a pretty big "or else" at the end of this verse: "or else I will come and strike the land with total destruction." God's intentions are clear: though the Old Testament begins with a family in dysfunction, and the narrative continues to exhibit dysfunctional families, God has in mind a plan to bring families together. If families resist this plan—if they live only for themselves, if they ignore or rebel against God's perfect design—the land will be cursed and the dysfunction will continue.

But if God's people are obedient, if they submit to God's work, parents will look to their children, and children will look to their parents. The parents will sacrifice for their children, and they'll remain faithful to their promise of marriage, because they know that a major purpose of marriage is to produce godly offspring. They'll realize godly kids are best raised in a stable, commitment-keeping environment, so they will work through their own marital challenges; they will want to give their kids the best chance to grow up as godly offspring. And in return, children will honor the message passed down to them from their parents, and they'll live in such a way that they'll pass this purpose down to their own children.

In our families, God invites us to present to the world a picture of the gospel message. My family is about so much more than me; it's about far more than whether my needs are getting met, my happiness is increasing, or my comfort is being accommodated. It's about preaching a truth by living it out. It's a mission, a calling, a heavy but glorious responsibility.

With each child comes a truly profound and awesome spiritual call. How will we respond? Will we pretend the call doesn't pertain to us, or will we soberly and humbly respond as Mary, the mother of Jesus, did when she approached parenting with the most perfect declaration imaginable: "I am the Lord's servant. . . . May your word to me be fulfilled" (Luke 1:38).

Do we have this attitude toward parenting—that we are the Lord's servant, eager to do as he bids? Are we humbly passionate and ready to faithfully fulfill our charge, raising a family that will point others to God and turn many from their sin? We need a daily reminder of this ultimate "why" of marriage and family life, lest we lose sight of the goal and lose motivation to keep making the right choices and sacrifices. It's so easy to coast, to just let the days slip by as we neglect the high call and hard work of sacred parenting.

In a Christmas morning devotion, I shared with my family about the faithful Rekabites, who served God when the rest of the Israelites wandered away. Though most in their neighborhoods and country had abandoned God, this faithful family stood true to a legacy of faith—and God noticed. In one of the most glorious promises in all of Scripture, God tells Jehonadab that he "will never fail to have a descendant to serve me" (Jeremiah 35:19).

What more soul-filling promise could a parent ever receive? That's the charge I gave to my son and two daughters: let's be a family that passes down our faith from generation to generation. Regardless of the spiritual climate in our culture, may we be a family that stays true to our spiritual heritage. May there always be a servant of God traced to our line until Jesus comes back. *Let's do our part to keep the gospel message alive.*

Parenting isn't just about changing diapers or trying to lure teens into a meaningful conversation; it's about a high and holy calling to raise children who honor and serve God. We are to be a family that invites the presence of Jesus into our hearts and homes, and in doing so we have the certain hope that he will invite *our* presence into his eternal home. Even more glorious, we live by the promise that perhaps he will, by his grace, also invite our descendants, down to the tenth or even twentieth generation. This is what, in Luther's words, "makes all suffering and labor worthwhile."[1]

Human history began with a wreck of a family—but it needn't end that way. By God's grace, we are invited to write a future history with the power and grace and guidance and comfort of the Messiah's Holy Spirit.

As we end this journey of looking at the spiritual side of parenting, let's consider what picture our families are giving to the world, and then join with God to more fully express the glory of his redemption.

Here's my last shot: Let's remember that parenting isn't about us—about our fulfillment, our joy, or even our pain; it's about *God*. It's about serving our Lord and being faithful to the calling he has laid at our feet, thereby proclaiming to the world God's merciful and glorious plan of redemption. Every decision we make as a family should be based on this call and this purpose. No, it's not an easy task. In fact, it may well be the most difficult task we ever undertake—but *that's* its glory. When you first became a parent, you may not have realized everything parenting involved, but now that we have a more complete picture, may we all pray, as Mary did, "I am the Lord's servant. May your word to me be fulfilled."

Let's finish strong and well, and let's wait for our reward.

*Heavenly Father, you have called us into the sacred journey of parenting. Help us to keep the end goal in mind: that family life is about proclaiming your truth to a broken world. Thank you for giving us such purpose and meaning. In Jesus' name, amen.*

## Questions for Reflection

1. How does God using such dysfunctional families in the Old Testament give us hope that he can use our imperfect families to advance his aims?

2. Discuss the added motivation of helping families to grow out of dysfunction so that others can see Jesus really and truly does make a difference in a family's life.

# NOTES

## Chapter 2: The Right Person for the Job

1. Charles Spurgeon, *Joy in Christ's Presence* (New Kensington, PA: Whitaker House, 1997), 103.
2. Ibid.
3. Ibid., 111–12.

## Chapter 3: A Lasting Mark

1. Andrew Murray, *Raising Your Children for Christ* (New Kensington, PA: Whitaker House, 1984), 121.
2. Ibid., 140.

## Chapter 5: Bring the Boy to Me

1. I'm indebted to Charles Spurgeon for his enlightening discussion of Obadiah in *Spiritual Parenting* (New Kensington, PA: Whitaker House, 1995), 141–54.
2. Cited in Dana Mack and David Blankenhorn, eds., *The Book of Marriage* (Grand Rapids: Eerdmans, 2001), 373.

## Chapter 9: The Song of the Childless Woman

1. William Martin, *Harvard Yard* (New York: Warner Books, 2003), 141.

## Chapter 10: Fear Factor

1. Spurgeon, *Joy in Christ's Presence*, 139.
2. Ibid., 140.
3. Ibid.
4. Ibid., 142.

## Chapter 11: Rude Is Rude

1. Judith Martin, *Miss Manners' Guide to Excruciatingly Correct Behavior* (New York: Atheneum, 1982), 49.

## Chapter 13: A Parent to Be Proud Of

1. Murray, *Raising Your Children for Christ*, 200.
2. Told in Richard Wurmbrand, *Tortured for Christ: 30th Anniversary Edition* (Bartlesville, OK: Living Sacrifice, 1998), 33–34.

## Chapter 14: Cut Down

1. Rachel Cusk, *A Life's Work: On Becoming a Mother* (New York: Picador, 2002), 55–56.
2. Cited in Rabbi Nancy Fuchs-Kreimer, *Parenting as a Spiritual Journey: Deepening Ordinary and Extraordinary Events into Sacred Occasions* (Woodstock, VT: Jewish Lights, 1998), 7.
3. Paul Evdokimov, *The Sacrament of Love* (Crestwood, NY: St. Vladimir's Seminary Press, 1985), 121.

## Chapter 16: I've Had My Turn

1. Cited in James Gorman, "Dog vs. Spouse," *New York Times Book Review* (June 1, 2003), 35.

## Chapter 17: Crushed Crayons

1. From an unpublished manuscript by Dr. Cathy Carpenter, shared with the author.
2. Ibid.

## Chapter 18: Hating Sin

1. Spurgeon, *Spiritual Parenting*, 144.

## Chapter 20: Humble Pie

1. Murray, *Raising Your Children for Christ*, 171.

## Chapter 22: Farsighted

1. Jonathan Edwards, *Heaven: A World of Love* (Amityville, NY: Calvary Press, 1999), 15.
2. Ibid.
3. Although I don't quote Andrew Murray directly, this devotion was inspired by some of his thoughts in *Raising Your Children for Christ*.

## Chapter 23: The Vice of the Virtuous

1. This and other quotes taken from Henry Drummond, *The Greatest Thing in the World* (London: Collins, 1930), 54–55.
2. Ibid.

## Chapter 24: Cursed Silence

1. Pat Conroy, *My Losing Season* (New York: Random House, 2002), 48.
2. Ibid.

## Chapter 27: A House of Love

1. Murray, *Raising Your Children for Christ*, 250.
2. Ibid., 276.
3. Spurgeon, *Spiritual Parenting*, 35–36.

## Chapter 28: The Eight-Pound Seminary Professor

1. Cited in Elysa Gardner, "Go-Go's, Bangles Pop into View," *USA Today* (May 18, 2001), 12E.
2. Cited in Mike Sager, "What I've Learned: Carrie Fisher," *Esquire* (January 2002), 97.
3. Cited in Lucy Kaylin, "The Rule of Law," *GQ* (July 2002), 124.

## Chapter 29: Be Tender, but Be True

1. Spurgeon, *Spiritual Parenting*, 176.
2. Ibid., 84.
3. Ibid.
4. Ibid., 106.
5. Ibid.

## Chapter 31: "Thanks for Stopping By"

1. Brandel Chamblee, "So Long, PGA Tour," *Sports Illustrated* (December 1, 2003), G11.
2. Ibid.
3. Ibid.

## Chapter 32: Cross Appointments

1. George Sayer, *Jack: C. S. Lewis and His Times* (San Francisco: Harper-San Francisco, 1988), 103.
2. Ibid.

## Chapter 35: Finger-Pointing

1. Jerry Sittser, *When God Doesn't Answer Your Prayer* (Grand Rapids: Zondervan, 2003), 163.
2. Ibid., 164.

## Chapter 37: Remember You'll Be Remembered

1. Cited in Gail Waesche Kislevitz, ed., *First Marathons* (Halcottsville, NY: Breakaway Books, 1999), 133.
2. Ibid., 169.

## Chapter 39: Treat 'Em Like Grandkids

1. Yona Zeldis McDonough, *The Four Temperaments* (New York: Doubleday, 2002), 293.
2. Blaise Pascal, *Pensees* (New York: Penguin, 1966), 43.

## Chapter 40: For the Kids

1. Jen Abbas, *Generation Ex: Adult Children of Divorce and the Healing of Our Pain* (Colorado Springs: Waterbrook, 2004), 1–2.
2. Ibid., 12.
3. Ibid., 12, 16.
4. Judith Wallerstein and Sandra Blakeslee, *Second Chances: Men, Women and Children a Decade After Divorce* (New York: Houghton Mifflin, 1996), 7
5. Abbas, *Generation Ex*, 18.
6. Ibid., 75.
7. Ibid., 19.
8. Ibid., 88.

## Chapter 43: Immortals in Our House

1. C. S. Lewis, *The Weight of Glory* (Grand Rapids: Eerdmans, 1949), 14–15, emphasis added.

## Chapter 44: Overwhelmed

1. Johann Christoph Arnold, *Sex, God and Marriage* (Farmington, PA: Plough, 2002), 73.

## Chapter 47: What You Were Born to Do

1. Cited in Mack and Blankenhorn, eds., *The Book of Marriage*, 369.
2. Ibid., 370.

## Chapter 52: A Picture Prophecy

1. Mack and Blankenhorn, 373.

# GARY THOMAS

*You can connect with Gary via his blog: www.garythomas.com/blog*
*Twitter: @garyLthomas*
*Facebook: www.facebook.com/authorgarythomas*

FOR INFORMATION ABOUT GARY'S MINISTRY AND HIS SPEAKING schedule, visit his website at www.garythomas.com. To inquire about inviting Gary to your church, please email Alli@garythomas.com, or make a request through our website.